Gerald

A PLACE TO STAND

A PLACE TO STAND

Elton Trueblood

PROFESSOR AT LARGE
EARLHAM COLLEGE

1817

HARPER & ROW, PUBLISHERS

NEW YORK, EVANSTON, AND LONDON

FIRST EDITION

LIBRARY OF CONGRESS CATALOG CARD NUMBERS 69-10474

M-S

To

Eli Lilly

who, because he has
found a place to
stand, has been able
to lift many burdens.

PREFACE

Because committed Christians are so obviously a minority today, it is important that they tell their neighbors what they believe and why. This book is my attempt to accept a portion of this responsibility. It represents the outcome of more than forty years of mental struggle. The book is, therefore, akin to autobiography, though it deals with ideas rather than with events. I have tried to express, forthrightly, the conclusions I have reached on the most important questions men can face, and I have tried, also, to explain the thinking processes which have led to these conclusions. My hope is that as a consequence readers, and particularly younger ones, will find something solid amidst the perplexities and confusions of the modern world.

As the careful reader will soon observe, my search for an honest answer to the deepest questions that perplex us has led me to a concrete faith which, for lack of a better term, may be called *Basic Christianity*. Though this can, I am convinced, be expressed in highly contemporary ways, it is no discovery of our age. I am well aware that the more "up to date" a book is, the sooner will it be dated. Though I am trying to speak to my own age, I hope that I am not overimpressed by it. If we discover anything which is really true, it will be equally true in succeeding centuries.

In the attempt to give the reader a frank explanation of the reasons that have led me to adopt a position which makes more sense than does any alternative known to me, I have tried to be clear. Part of the shame of the theology of the recent past is that sometimes it has been made deliberately foggy, under the fatuous assumption that what cannot be understood is somehow more profound. Because the chief secret of clarity is that of logical order, the sequence of topics is of the first importance. Therefore the order of chapters in this book is meant to reflect the order of thought.

Though by faith I am a Christian, by profession I am a philosopher, and I have tried to remember the latter while writing of the former. Always, as I write, I try to keep in mind the arduous standard which my teacher, Professor Arthur O. Lovejoy, demonstrated and expected. After his death, one of his former students said, "With his eyes upon you, you would weigh your words twice before uttering them. His presence discouraged laxity of thought, intellectual bravado, and facile talking."[1] Because the issues are of such magnitude the philosopher, when he shares his thoughts on the Christian faith, must set for himself standards which are not less, but even more rigorous, than those expected in other areas of intellectual inquiry.

Ever since I first encountered the mind of Blaise Pascal I have been intrigued by his ambitious purpose. Day after day he gathered notes for a book he hoped to write, in which he would try to tell the ordinary thoughtful seeker why he had found a center of stability in the midst of his perplexity. My book, of course, is far different from the one Pascal would have written had he lived to complete his self-appointed task,

[1] Ludwig Edelstein, "In Memory of A. O. Lovejoy," *Journal of the History of Ideas*. Vol. XXIV, No. 4, p. 451.

but the purpose is the same. My hope is that the book will be of assistance to the ordinary seeker who is trying to be intellectually honest.

D. E. T.

Earlham College
Labor Day, 1968

CONTENTS

CHAPTER I

RATIONAL CHRISTIANITY

———————◆———————

Give me a place to stand and I will move the earth.
—ARCHIMEDES

Though human life is always paradoxical, the sharpness of
the paradox has been accentuated in our generation. Consequently, we are forced to employ apparent opposites in order
to describe our time with any accuracy. The words with
which Charles Dickens began *A Tale of Two Cities* were
meant to apply to the period of the French Revolution, but
they apply equally now, for the famous opening, "It was the
best of times; it was the worst of times," has an astonishingly
contemporary ring. Fantastic successes in some areas of human experience are now balanced by radical failures in
others. Sometimes both the success and the failure appear in
the same individual life.

The paradox of the greatness and the littleness of man to
which Pascal gave brilliant expression more than three hundred years ago is now demonstrated for all to see. The greatness, which is exemplified in many ways, is especially obvious
in technology. Not all believe that we should use our energies
to put a man on the moon, but no one can fail to be impressed by the skill required in placing men in orbit. This
could not have been accomplished without a very high level

of competence and loyal teamwork. Yet, at the same time, the despair in millions of minds is equally striking.

Many terms can be applied to our age, but one of the most accurate affirmations is that ours has become an age of confusion, in which people simply do not know what to think. Part of this is the result of bitter disappointment. Technology has not brought Utopia; the Great Society has not emerged; peace is as elusive as ever; poverty still exists. In no area is the perplexity greater than in that of religious belief. Millions, including large sections of the nominal membership of the churches, are without any firm conviction on which to base and rebuild their lives. It is common to hear men say that, while they once believed in God in a deeply personal sense, they do so no longer. The consequence is spiritual emptiness, a most dangerous situation. Not only is the old faith for many completely gone; there is nothing to take its place. Regardless of what statistics may report, committed Christians are today a minority, not only in Asia, but also in western Europe and in North America. To face this as a fact, and to act accordingly, is the responsibility of all who are willing to follow the path of realism.

A quarter of a century ago a few of us began to say that faith in the possibility of a cut-flower civilization is a faith which is bound to fail.[1] What we meant was that it is impossible to sustain certain elements of human dignity, once these have been severed from their cultural roots. The sorrowful fact is that, while the cut flowers seem to go on living and may even exhibit some brightness for a while, they cannot do so permanently, for they will eventually wither and be discarded. The historical truth is that the chief sources of the concepts of the dignity of the individual and equality before the law are found in the Biblical heritage. Apart from the

---

[1] My own contribution to this theme appeared in *The Predicament of Modern Man* (New York: Harper & Row, 1944), pp. 59 ff.

fundamental convictions of that heritage, symbolized by the idea that every man is made in the image of God, there is no adequate reason for accepting the concepts mentioned. Since human beings are often far from admirable in their actual behavior, man's dignity is fundamentally derivative in nature.

No satisfaction comes to any student of the philosophy of civilization from the fact that a sad prediction is coming true, but verification of the above is increasingly obvious. Part of the meaning of our contemporary confusion is that the effort to create and to maintain a cut-flower civilization is already failing. We can point, indeed, to some acts of compassion, and we exhibit some courage, but the withering is a fact, for on all sides there is a loss of confidence. The machines are bright, but the faces of the people are not as bright as the machines they prize and struggle to purchase. Perhaps even the brightness of the machines will eventually fade, since their continued production depends, not merely on technical skill, but even more upon the trustworthiness of their makers and designers.

Always men have broken laws; that is nothing new. What is new is the acceptance of a creed to the effect that there really is no objective truth about what human conduct ought to be. The new position is not merely that the old laws do not apply, but rather that *any* moral law is limited to subjective reference. While this has been the position of a few individuals in various generations of the past, our time differs markedly in that this has suddenly become the position of millions. Some of them still have a slight connection with the Judeo-Christian heritage, but the obvious conflict in convictions will, if it continues, finally dissolve even the mild connection that still appears to exist. If there is no objective right, then there is not even the possibility of error, and intellectual and moral confusion are bound to ensue. The most frightening aspect of this situation is the degree to

which it renders the masses vulnerable to some new dogmatism which may arise. This will not be Hitlerism, since
that has been fully discredited, but something like it may
again succeed if the people have nothing better than their
own subjective whims to oppose to the new creed. After all,
Hitler had his own "thing."

Among those who have analyzed our contemporary moral
predicament, none has been more incisive than America's
best-known Jewish philosopher, Will Herberg, Graduate Professor of Philosophy and Culture at Drew University. Professor Herberg does not merely tell how bad the situation is;
he analyzes it in depth. His major conclusions have appeared
in an article entitled "What Is the Moral Crisis of Our
Time?" The author is keenly aware that the crisis is something deeper than the war in Vietnam, or the race riots, or
crime in the streets. The trouble, he points out, seems to
come not from the breaking of moral laws but from something far more serious: the rejection of the conception that
there is any moral law at all. The danger, as Herberg sees it,
is not merely lying, which we have always had, but the meaninglessness of the very concept of truth. "The moral crisis of
our time," Herberg concludes, "consists not so much in the
violation of standards generally accepted as in the attrition,
to the point of irrelevance, of these very standards themselves."[2] What makes Herberg's thesis radically different from
what is usually said about the moral crisis is his recognition
that we have something on our hands very much more serious
than we have ordinarily supposed. Failure to honor particular moral standards is one thing; rejection of the very idea of
an objective moral standard is another.

As we analyze our moral situation, noting that the new
position which Will Herberg describes is becoming ever
more fashionable, we must understand that the consequent

2 *The Intercollegiate Review,* Vol. 4 (March, 1968) , p. 65.

predicament is not a simple one. Part of the oddity is that many people who, on one side of their lives, conclude that there is no moral order to which they owe allegiance as human beings, still retain some capacity for moral outrage. It should be noted that most protests are couched in terms of moral indignation, though they are sometimes made by people who claim to reject all moral requirements in their own lives. Theoretical moral indifference is coupled with actual moral condemnation of others, couched in absolute terms. If we were consistent this would not be the case; but we are not consistent. Some who reject any possibility of objective reference in moral judgments are still shocked by murder. Probably we ought to look upon this inconsistency as a sign of hope, indicating that people may be better in their personal conduct than in their philosophy. The taxi driver who boasts that he will do anything to get ahead, and that he has no moral principles, may in practice be scrupulous about his reading of the meter even when the passenger cannot see it.

The greatest single benefit to our contemporary civilization may come, not from some new invention, but from the reinvigoration of the roots which have, at various periods, produced cultural flowers almost universally admired. Though these roots have been shamefully neglected, they are not dead, and with sufficient thought they may be made productive again. At least, since there is a chance of success, we are driven to the effort by the revelation of the unsatisfactory character of all known alternatives. Millions now assume, without argument, that the Biblical view of life is obsolete, but it is conceivable that they are wrong. It is the deepest conviction of the author of this book that they *are* wrong!

Part of the weakness of the Christian movement in our generation has been the relative lack of emphasis upon belief. There are three areas that must be cultivated if any faith is to be a living faith: the inner life of devotion, the intellectual life of rational thought, and the outer life of human service. There is no doubt as to which of these has been most neglected in our time; it is the emphasis upon rational belief. Christian books dealing with prayer and worship have been plentiful; books urging men and women to tasks of mercy have been abundant; but good books helping people to arrive at sound convictions have been scarce. Even some which would appear to be concerned with belief only succeed in repeating the questions by which people are already disturbed, rather than in providing any clear answers. Popular preachers stay very close to social issues and avoid involvement in the problems of ultimate faith. Yet it is a revealing fact that when men such as John Stott, rector of All Souls' Church in London, have the courage and wisdom to engage in an affirmative approach to Basic Christianity they receive a tremendous hearing, particularly from the young.

However good and important human service is, it loses its motive power when the sustaining beliefs are allowed to wither. That mere humanistic idealism has a natural tendency to end in bitterness is not really surprising. People *do* disappoint us, and if we have nothing more fundamental upon which to depend than the natural goodness of man we are bound to end in a mood of futility. The social witness of the modern Church, especially in regard to racial justice, is very important, but we need to remember that the social gospel depends ultimately upon convictions. Unless it is true that each person, regardless of race or sex, is one who is made in the image of the Living God, much of the impetus of work for social justice is removed. Such work may go on for a generation, by social momentum, but it will not continue much longer. The "slip carriage" detached from its engine finally comes to a full stop. Social momentum is not permanent.

The rejection of creeds in the modern Christian Church is easily understandable It is a fact that the words of both the Apostles' and the Nicene Creed seem to many in our generation merely antique, having lost their power by constant repetition. But confusion arises when people move from an antipathy toward particular creeds to rejection of all creedal expression, for then the woeful result is that they have nothing upon which to build their lives.

There is really no hope for the Christian faith apart from tough-mindedness in matters of belief. If God is not, then the sooner we find it out the better. If belief in God is not true, it is an evil and should be eliminated from our entire universe of discourse. False belief is evil because it diverts energy from practical tasks that require attention. If prayer is not an objective encounter with the Living God, we shall do well to make this discovery and give up the nonsense as soon as possible.

We hear, repeatedly, the cliché that deeds are everything while beliefs are unimportant; but this is manifest nonsense. The truth is that belief leads to action, and acting often depends upon believing. We are wise to remind ourselves of what Dr. Johnson said to Boswell on July 14, 1763, apropos of a man who denied the existence of a moral order: "If he does really think that there is no distinction between virtue and vice, why, Sir, when he leaves our house, let us count our spoons."[3] If men believe that slaves are not fully human they will treat them as they treat animals. A man who is convinced that something is impossible will not, if he is intelligent, try to produce it.

Unfortunately, the intellectual effort that modern man so desperately needs, especially in his faith, is not being generally encouraged. Instead, there is a real discouragement

3 James Boswell, *The Life of Samuel Johnson* (New York: John B. Alden, 1887), Vol. I. p. 346.

produced by the preaching of anti-intellectualism. What we hear and read, over and over, is that the existence of God cannot be proved. The consequence is that many draw the erroneous conclusion that all items of faith are devoid of intellectual support. Since men certainly will not seek what they are convinced they cannot have, the effort to develop a reasoned faith is naturally not even attempted. Examples of abdication in the face of rational difficulty are easy to find, not only among average churchmen, but also among religious leaders. Jospeh Fletcher subscribes with charming simplicity to the anti-intellectualist creed, and with no qualification, when he concludes that "philosophy is utterly useless as a way to bridge the gap between doubt and faith."[4] A similar position is expressed by the pastor of Judson Church in New York when he describes the new mood in the congregation which he guides. "The Judson people," he says proudly, "are learning to live in a world of the withering away of apologetics."[5]

What we need desperately, at this particular juncture in the enduring human crisis, is the emergence of Christian intellectuals. If Basic Christianity is to survive, it must be served by a highly dedicated and highly trained group of persons who are unabashed and unapologetic in the face of opposition and ridicule. They must be able to outthink as well as outlive all attacks on the central faith which we so sorely need as an alternative to confusion. Because this has been possible in many other generations of need, there is good reason to believe that it is possible again. Professor Pelikan has pointed out what is sometimes forgotten: that the leaders of the Reformation were themselves keen intellectuals. He refers to men of the stature of Calvin as "a cadre of

---

[4] Joseph Fletcher, *Situation Ethics* (Philadelphia: Westminster Press, 1966), p. 41.

[5] Howard Moody in *Who's Killing the Church?* (Chicago: Church Missionary Society, 1960), p. 87.

intellectuals."[6] Being himself an example as well as an exponent of Christian intellectualism, Professor Pelikan deserves to be heard.

It is not hard to see how popular anti-intellectualism has arisen. It is a revolt against the kind of rationalism represented by St. Thomas Aquinas, which some say may convince the mind but not the heart. Furthermore, many are vaguely aware of the criticisms of the traditional arguments for the existence of God in the work of Immanual Kant and his successors. But as so often occurs in the history of human thought, the tendency is to fall into an extreme even worse than the one that is being rejected. This has, in fact, occurred in our time. However bad some arid intellectualism has been, anti-intellectualism is worse, since it provides no antidote to either superstition or wish-thinking. If the tough-minded concern for evidence and for consistency is given up, there is no way to detect error, or even to distinguish between degrees of probability. Archbishop Temple touched exactly the right note when he pointed out that "the most important of mental disciplines for almost all purposes is not that which distinguishes between certainty and probability, but that which leads to discrimination between degrees of probability."[7]

The familiar statement that God cannot be proved is fundamentally ambiguous. On one hand it may mean that the existence of the One whom Christ called Father cannot be proved beyond a shadow of a doubt, but on the other hand it may mean, and often does mean, that there is no valid evidence for the being of God. One does not need to be a professional philosopher to see that these two meanings differ

6 Jaroslav Pelikan, *The Christian Intellectual* (New York: Harper & Row, 1965) , p. 17.

7 William Temple, *Nature, Man and God* (London: Macmillan & Co., 1934) , p. 84.

radically. Part of the trouble lies in the fact that, while the writer may mean the first, the reader may interpret him as meaning the second, with the result that faith is further eroded.

The time has now come to point out that the sentence, "God cannot be proved," while true, is profoundly misleading. Furthermore, it is often used in a way which is manifestly dishonest, because care is not taken to add that absolute proof is not possible anywhere else. Without the addition of this important observation, the reader is not to be blamed if he concludes, erroneously, that items of Christian faith are without support while items in other fields, such as science, have the value of *certainty*.

It is now widely recognized that absolute proof is something which the human being does not and cannot have.[8] This follows necessarily from the twin fact that deductive reasoning cannot have certainty about its premises and that inductive reasoning cannot have certainty about its conclusions. The notion that, in natural science, we have both certainty and absolute proof is simply one of the superstitions of our age. We have, of course, high probability, but that is a different matter. Even in the first great burst of scientific reasoning, in what Alfred North Whitehead called "the century of genius," it was already recognized that absolute proof is not given to finite minds. Thus Blaise Pascal asked his fellow scientists, "Who has demonstrated that there will be a tomorrow, and that we shall die?"[9] He knew that all science depends upon assumptions which are incapable of proof.

Once we face honestly the fact that complete demonstration is not within our scope, we are in a far better situation

---

[8] I have dealt with this in an entire chapter (Chap. V) entitled "The Limits of Proof," in my *General Philosophy* (New York: Harper & Row, 1963).

[9] *Pensées*, No. 252.

to do what we *can* do. Whether we are considering the existence of God or the existence of atoms, we need not, because we lack certainty, give up the effort to *believe honestly,* for though nothing is supported perfectly, some items of faith are far better supported than others. The horoscope predictions which still appear in our newspapers are not based upon any evidence which will bear full examination, whereas the conclusions of modern astronomy are supported by abundant and cumulative evidence. The way of wisdom is not to give up the effort to believe when we recognize that absolute certainty is denied us, but rather to recognize degrees of evidential value. The practical danger of all perfectionism is that it leads so easily to abandonment of the comparative good which *is* possible. Though we may never know, in this life, the absolute truth about anything, we have sufficient evidence on which to proceed, and we can at least rid our minds of frauds.

The greatest danger that comes from frequent repetition of the phrase, "God cannot be proved," is that it lodges in the public mind the idea that reason has nothing to do with the matter at all. This leads millions to the impotence of mere "fideism." The word means acceptance of "faith alone," with no concern for intellectual content. The crucial difficulty of this position, however popular it may be at times, is that it provides no means of *choosing between* radically different faiths. It gives no basis for rejecting the Nazi faith or even the faith of voodooism. Once the life of reason is rejected, there is no reason why any one faith is better or worse than any other. The pathetic fact is that the people who say they do not need to give reasons for the objective validity of the faith they espouse do not seem to realize how sad the consequences of their position are.

The current rejection of apologetics is both misguided and futile, for it abandons the citadel to the enemy. Even the harshest critic of Basic Christianity has no objection to the affirmation of a faith which cannot defend itself before thoughtful minds, since he can afford to be tolerant of anything so weak, because he is fundamentally contemptuous. Accordingly, one of the most urgent tasks of contemporary Christians is to express a faith which can be made credible for modern man. Enthusiasm is not enough! It will do something for a while, but it will soon evaporate unless the faith which is espoused can be so stated that those who do not share the enthusiasm can be convinced in their minds.[10] No faith can survive unless it meets the double test of intellectual validity and social relevance.

Few tasks are more important for Christians now than that of a reconsideration of the function of reason. We need to try to understand what reason can do and what it cannot. One of the most brilliant observations of Plato concerned what he called "misology," which he said was the worst thing that can happen to a man. The misologist is a person who, having become discouraged by his inability in dialectics, concludes that careful reasoning has no value. By this step he succeeds in transferring the blame from himself and his own ineptitude; but he undermines, at the same time, any possibility of detecting error. "Let us then, in the first place," said Plato, "be careful of allowing or of admitting into our souls the notion that there is no health or soundness in any arguments at all."[11] Accepting Plato's estimate of the radical nature of this evil, Wayne Booth, Dean of the College of the University of Chicago, expresses his fear that the disease has already fastened upon us. "How else," he asks, "can we explain the fact that, in an institution devoted to learning and supported

[10] A vivid illustration of this process is provided by the history of Quakerism in the seventeenth century. The movement of George Fox and his contemporaries was saved from the dismal fate of similar movements by the brilliant work of Robert Barclay. Even Voltaire was impressed!

[11] Plato, *Phaedo*, 90E.

by the public for that purpose, the words of a speaker are so drowned by raucous noises that no one even hears what is being said?" The sad consequence is that there is no chance of examining the proposal the speaker has come to make. Dean Booth makes the startling suggestion that, in fifty years, his words about the importance of reason may not even be understood.[12]

Though reason is necessary to the Christian faith, it is probable that most people are not, in fact, drawn to a full faith by intellectual arguments. While the late T. S. Eliot was so drawn, it must be admitted that he was exceptional. Can you by searching find out God? (Job 11:7) is still a question to which the answer is presumably negative. But if we end at this point we are missing important elements of practical significance. One of the chief of these is that strict honesty in reasoning may help immensely in answering objections to the faith that is centered in Jesus Christ. Though reason alone may not enable men to find God, it can do wonders in enabling them to surmount serious barriers to the achievement of an examined faith.

A graduate student in a leading American university asked one of his philosophy professors, who was not a Christian, whether his studies in philosophy would help him to see the truth of his Christian faith. The professor after answering that these studies would not have this effect, then added, "Your studies will do something that is equally important. They will enable you to answer the attacks upon the faith. Your opponents are more vulnerable than you or they realize." The professor's observation is similar to that of Coleridge, whose understanding of the function of reason in religion has not been given the attention it deserves. "Reason," wrote Coleridge, "becomes an effective ally by exposing

12 Booth's article was reprinted in the Wall Street Journal for February 14, 1968.

the false show of demonstration, or by evincing the equal demonstrability of the contrary from premises equally logical."[13]

The way to be a nonconformist today is to revive the heritage of "obstinate rationality" represented by Socrates and Samuel Johnson. This can be especially powerful if it is joined by the use of humor, including the ability to laugh at oneself and one's own pretensions. Though the tough use of reason does not assure attainment of all of the answers, it at least makes us aware of questions not otherwise raised. Reason does not make us wholly free from mistakes, but it is wonderfully effective in making us *detect* the mistakes we make. Recognition of error is really, therefore, our major ground of hope of rationality. However hard it may be to be *right,* we can see, in many instances, where we are wrong!

As we try to find our way through the confusion of a period in which many are convinced that there is no dependable point of trust, it is helpful to recognize our middle position as finite minds. We are equally separated from absolute certainty about the truth and from absolute ignorance of it. Pascal clarified our middle state when he wrote, "Now there is, humanly speaking, no certainty, but we have reason."[14] Part of our dignity lies in the fact that we can be aware of our necessary humility. Though no belief about the world is entirely demonstrable, the claim that we have nothing on which to depend in not a logical consequence of our fallibility.

By a reaffirmation of the possibility of reason we have a practical approach to the mystery that surrounds us, because we can at least require of our opinions both consistency and coherence. Consistency does not mean unwillingness to grow

13 Samuel Taylor Coleridge, *Biographia Literatia* (London: J. M. Dent & Sons, 1906) , p. 106.
14 *Pensées,* No. 822.

or to learn in the light of new evidence; it means, rather, the unwillingness to say out of one side of one's mouth what is denied on the other side. A lack of concern for consistency is, in the intellectual enterprise, indecent. For example, it is indecent to demand of religious truth a level of certainty which is not demanded of scientific truth. It is a double standard, destructive of integrity.

The more rational we become the more we are concerned for the objectivity of truth. The same proposition cannot be true for one man and false for another, because then the confusion would be intrinsic and the effort to know the truth would be a meaningless undertaking. Here the clarification provided by Alec Vidler is particularly helpful. Speaking of the Christian faith, Vidler has written, "Either it is true for all men, whether they know it or not; or it is true for no one, not even for those people who are under the illusion that it is true."[15] Though the subjective judgment of any individual man or group of men may be mistaken, it is essential to the life of reason to recognize that there is something which the individual or the group is mistaken *about*. What men are mistaken about is what we mean when we refer to the truth, regardless of the character of the inquiry. What we must do, as finite persons, is to try to improve our methods of inquiry so that, whether we are speaking of atoms or of the Living God, we can be brought progressively closer to knowing what is, in distinction to what we happen to desire. "I prefer to believe" is an un-Christian sentence.

All modern philosoply began with the decision of Descartes to try, by the method of systematic doubt, to detect whatever is doubtful and consequently reject it in any field of inquiry. Helpful as the Cartesian decision was, we can now see that the famous thinker overstated his position. Partly

---

15 Alec Vidler, *Christian Belief* (London: SCM Press, 1950), p. 10.

because of the thinking of his younger French contemporary, Blaise Pascal, we are more keenly aware than Descartes of the fact that life presents us with forced options in which there is some doubt associated with each alternative. The complete elimination of doubt is therefore intrinsically impossible. The way forward, in such cases, is not that of looking for a position in connection with which there is no doubt at all, but rather of accepting the alternative in which the elements of doubt are *fewer*. The complete acceptance of the formula of Descartes would, in fact, make the employment of practical reason impossible. We may speak lightly of "beyond a shadow of a doubt," but this is not what we find in actual experience.

The recognition that the function of reason is largely involved in the comparison of difficulties is one of the major steps in philosophical thinking. Though the idea applies to the whole of philosophy, the thinkers of the twentieth century who have expressed it most eloquently are both theologians. These are H. G. Wood, of the University of Birmingham, and John Baillie, of the University of Edinburgh. Both men reported the immense intellectual relief which they experienced when they realized that it is not wise to give up a position when it seems to involve difficulties, unless it is possible to find an alternative position that exhibits less serious difficulties. There are, for example, serious difficulties associated with the conviction that there is life after death, some of them having to do with the problem of how consciousness is possible subsequent to the physical decay of the brain, but a person of any intellectual maturity is also aware that there are equally serious or even greater difficulties attending the conviction that the death of the flesh is the end of the human story. Some of these difficulties will be presented in Chapter V of this book. The point here is that it is unduly simplistic to reject any position without a careful examination of its alternatives. Serious as are the problems of Christian belief, the problems of unbelief may be even more serious. In a world in which no logical case is ever perfect, it is nevertheless a mistake to choose the less perfect; though no evidence is ever watertight, some leaks are smaller than others!

A new day is dawning for Christian intellectuals who will prepare themselves for the arduous and much-needed task of helping their fellows to cut through the fog and confusion that mark the climate of current opinion. Too many Christians who might reasonably be looked upon as intellectuals have settled for a confessional posture and are no longer challenging the critics. An effective attack is possible, however, precisely because the enemies of the faith are themselves so obviously vulnerable. C. S. Lewis was highly successful as a Christian intellectual who followed such a course,[16] but the shame is that he was so nearly alone and that he has so few contemporary successors.

Much of the fear of the role of the intellectual arises from the false assumption that a presentation of the basic faith in rational terms involves, at the same time, a loss of warmth and affection. To know that this is not necessary we need only look at the life of John Baillie, who combined the affectionate faith of a little child with the tough mentality of a highly civilized man. In one of the books which Mrs. Baillie has released since her husband's death, the biographical note tells how three objects in the great man's study were symbolic of the wholeness of his career. One was the desk where he wrote, a second was the chair where he read, and the third was the pad where, daily, he knelt to pray.[17] More than most thinkers, Baillie is a model for our time of need.

When the enemies of reason seek allies they frequently

16 Lewis first made people pay attention when, in the *Screwtape Letters*, he challenged the bland assumption that unbelievers have a monopoly on intelligence.

17 John Baillie, *Christian Devotion* (New York: Charles Scribner's Sons, 1962) , pp. 15, 16.

quote the familiar words of Pascal, "The heart has its reasons, which reason does not know,"[18] but in this they are making a serious mistake. Pascal, being himself an unusually keen rationalist, is not their ally. When he contrasts the reasons of the heart with the reasons of the head he is not denying reason, but instead is seeking to show the necessity of the involvement of the entire person. In saying that reason, as ordinarily understood, is not all there is, he is not denying but rather supplementing it. "We know truth," he said, "not only by the reason, but also by the heart."[19] Pascal would have been the last man to make a defense of unreason or to encourage misology.

In T. S. Eliot's examination of Pascal's method we find something of a model of what the procedure of the Christian intellectual should be. Pascal, says Eliot, looks at as much of the world as he can see and proceeds by rejection and elimination. He finds in the world as observed that which is inexplicable on a nontheistic basis and proceeds to a conclusion, not as a dogmatist, but as an intelligent seeker trying to make sense of his world. "Now Pascal's method," wrote Eliot, "is the method natural and right for the Christian."[20] In this I heartily concur. Pascal has become our teacher because he was explaining to himself the sequence that culminated in his vital faith. He was not, regardless of the proposed name of his book, the public apologist, but primarily the reporter. What we desperately need is the literature of witness in which men who have reached a firm place to stand are able to tell us the road by which they have come and why it was taken. We need a whole new group of thinkers who are willing and able to obey the injunction of I Peter 3:15, being prepared to make

18 *Pensées,* No. 277.
19 *Pensées,* No. 282.
20 T. S. Eliot, in the Introduction to *Pascal's Pensées* (London: J. M. Dent & Sons, 1931), p. xii.

a defense of the "hope that is in them," but doing it "with gentleness and reverence." The result may be that the word apology will lose its present connotations.

Unless a new group of Christian intellectuals can arise, our prospect is a dreary one. The hope of any real guidance from professional philosophers, the natural expectation in other generations, is extremely doubtful. This is true, not primarily because of a dearth of able men, but because contemporary philosophy has been so largely directed to questions which are essentially trivial. The essence of the failure lies not in the character of the answers given, some of which are true, but rather in the character of the questions asked.

Finally we are witnessing the verification of Whitehead's prediction of failure in the midst of advance. "The dawn of brilliant epochs," he said, "is shadowed by the massive obscurantism of human nature."[21] Once, large sections of the clergy were the standard examples of obscurantism, but today their places have been taken by the academic philosophers. Whatever else academic philosophy may do in our generation, it is improbable that it will provide desperate men and women with a firm place to stand in the face of the present confusion and perplexity about values. Indeed, the forfeiture of values is one of the saddest elements in the plight of the big universities, and the departments of philosophy must bear a large measure of responsibility for this development. The intellectuals we need will necessarily stand in the heritage of Socrates and Pascal rather than in that of Protagoras and Montaigne.

The Christian intellectual provides our best hope because he has access to both the reasons of the heart and the reasons of the head, and if he is worthy of his vocation he knows how to combine them. He can hold in one context

21 Alfred North Whitehead, *The Function of Reason* (Boston: Beacon Press, 1958), p. 43.

both intellectual integrity and depth of spiritual experience, with no sense of incompatibility. In short, he can both pray and think! He will be keenly aware of the appeals of both agnosticism and dogmatism, but he will resist both, because both represent escape from the struggle for an intelligent faith. What we need is thoughtful people who belong to the fellowship of perplexity, yet have discovered points of clarity in the midst of the confusion. This is the strategy of Basic Christianity. We do not have certainty in the absolute sense Descartes sought, but we have a commitment which provides a starting point for all else. It is a mark of maturity to believe fewer doctrines, but to believe them with greater intensity.

In presenting Basic Christianity to seekers, it is particularly important to avoid the use of labels and artificial classifications. It is pointless to try to pigeonhole a man as a "liberal" or an "evangelical," for every sound Christian is both of these. He is an evangelical because he has settled one question: he is Christ-centered. But he is also a liberal because he is willing to learn from any source and to face new truth whenever and wherever it is revealed. How inept it is to suppose that a man is either a philosopher or one who accepts revelation, is made obvious when we consider the life and thought of William Temple of Canterbury. Temple was a big enough man to have more than one side to his life, and he combined them with éclat.

For the most part theological labels serve no useful purpose, because they tend to classify what cannot be classified without distortion. Labels, instead of encouraging thought, have the effect of diminishing it in that once a man's classification is known, there seems to be no need of further inquiry. Thus, when we call a man a conservative theologian, we feel that we can safely limit his influence to his particular party. Conservatism is not, however, the mark of a party, but something essential to the life of every thoughtful person. All intelligent people are conservatives, because they seek to conserve the accumulated wisdom of mankind. They are keenly aware of the fact that we are not rich enough in human resources to waste anything of tested value. But in the same way, every Christian theologian is radical in that he wants to go to the root of the matter. He is not willing to settle for mere priestcraft or ceremonial, and like Socrates he is willing to follow the evidence wherever it may lead. Only by a combination of conservatism and radicalism is progress possible. The people who are willing to end discussion by employing the old labels merely demonstrate that they have not caught up with the modern world.

The fallacy of easy classification is that of supposing that tendencies represent separate men, when in fact they usually represent competing elements within the lives of individual men. Almost every thinking person has a more or less continuous dialogue within his own consciousness. Though it is a mistake to settle for party tags, it is not a mistake to speak of competing tendencies. When we learn that Barth refuses to be considered a Barthian, we begin to understand that no great thinker is ever satisfied to be restricted to one classification. Such an example makes it necessary to point out that, when we use terms ending in "ism," as is sometimes necessary, we are speaking more of tendencies than of groups of men.

In spite of all the variations of Christian belief, there has normally been, and there is now, a central stream of thought. What we denote as Basic Christianity is that which exists at the center of the Christian spectrum. Far from being sectarian, it is represented in nearly all denominations. This central stream is both rational and evangelical. The essential feature is commitment to Jesus Christ, who told His followers to love God with all their minds (Mark 12:30).

While there are many current evidences of decay, there is also a saving remnant, especially among those of the silent center. In spite of the much-publicized erosion of faith, large segments of our people accept Christ as the surest reality of their lives; they truly love God, and they engage in service to their fellow men which is motivated by this love. The strange fact, however, is that the vast majority of contemporary Christians have no adequate voice, because they have so few spokesmen to whom the intellectual world is willing to listen. The tendency is to give major attention, and the headlines, to faddists. We must develop spokesmen who are able to articulate the faith of the great body of Christians who, though they seldom speak up, are tremendously important.

The two great words of Christian history are *evangelical* and *catholic*. Both are so precious that it is a serious mistake to use them merely to refer to parties or denominations. Neither term should ever be permitted to become the monopoly or private possession of a single group, since each is too big for that! The reason why every genuine Christian is catholic is that Christ's call is universal. We are called to be the salt, not merely of a little group, but of the whole earth. In the same way every genuine Christian is evangelical, because a Christian is one who answers affirmatively the call, "Come to me" (Matthew 11:28). This book is one man's honest attempt to show how it is possible to be both catholic and evangelical, as we go deeper into our century of storm.

A major problem is how Basic Christianity can be presented as a live option for our troubled time without seeming to run off an old record which people will dismiss because they suppose it is familiar. Actually, of course, there are millions for whom it is not familiar, but this they do not know. Most people, including those outside the Church, suppose that they are acquainted with the teachings of Christ as reported in the Gospels, but in this many are self-deluded, since they have never read a word of the Biblical account.

We are not likely to get very many of these people, who are the most characteristic of our time, to read the New Testament because the dogma of its irrelevance to their problems is unquestioned. What is conceivable, however, is that a good many may be open to an approach which stresses logical thinking. Even an elementary acquaintance with the new mathematics provides an understanding of the process of implication. Having long supposed that religion is merely a matter of emotion, some may be pleasantly surprised to face a basic proposition, along with its major implications. The key to the logic of belief lies in finding a firm place from which to operate. Since the necessity of such a starting point has long been recognized in both mathematics and science, it is reasonable that the same should be true in dealing with the questions that affect human life most deeply. Every set of logically connected propositions leads us back finally to some primitive proposition. The primary proposition for the Christian, his ultimate act of faith, is *the trustworthiness of Jesus Christ*. It is here that the Christian finds a place to stand. Because of this logical structure, the epigraph of this chapter is the famous affirmation of Archimedes.[22] Being the inventor of both the lever and the pulley, Archimedes seemed to the king of Syracuse and his other contemporaries able to accomplish wonders, but there was, he said, one necessary condition. The fulcrum had to be firm.

Readers who appreciate Thomas Carlyle are likely to remember the remarkable contrast which Carlyle made between Johnson and Hume. The lives of the two British intellectual

---

22 For the context of the affirmation in the life and thought of Archimedes, see Plutarch, *Life of Marcellus*.

giants of the eighteenth century were so truly contemporary that each reminds us of the other. It was part of the genius of Carlyle to see that, great as these thinkers were, they were both half-men. Hume saw the difficulties of belief so keenly that he never became a Christian; Johnson felt the difficulties of unbelief so keenly that he had no respect for the unbeliever. "They were the two half-men of their time: whoso should combine the intrepid candour and decisive scientific clearness of Hume with the Reverence, the Love and devout Humility of Johnson, were the whole men of our time."[23]

I have no doubt that, though David Hume and Samuel Johnson were both half-men, Johnson's was the superior half. Indeed, Johnson exhibited more intellectual clarity than even Carlyle realized. But it is the combination that we must seek with all the care we are able to muster. In any case, we must not settle for anything less. Since the supposition that we must choose between clear-mindedness and reverence is something that has no foundation in fact, the rational evangelical is the new man for our generation. It is the vocation of the Christian intellectual to be both tough-minded and tender-minded, and to be both at once.

[23] Thomas Carlyle, *Critical and Miscellaneous Essays* (New York: Charles Scribner's Sons, 1904), Vol. III, p. 135.

CHAPTER II

A CENTER OF CERTITUDE

I shall be entitled to entertain the highest expectations, if I am fortunate enough to discover only one thing that is certain and indubitable.

—RENÉ DESCARTES

It is not easy to know the right order to employ in the effort to assist modern man in reaching an alternative to confusion and futility. While there is much that is worth saying, it will not be accepted or even understood unless it appears in a sequence that makes sense to contemporary seekers. How well Pascal understood this when he planned the great intellectual effort of his life is shown by Pensée 19: "The last thing one settles in writing a book is what one should put in first."

The usual procedure in the development of a theology is to present, first of all, a discussion of God. Though this seems natural and is, of course, supported by the order of the famous creeds, it will not suffice today, for if modern man is to be reached, it must be in a radically different fashion. To begin with God, Maker of heaven and earth, is indeed to follow the logical order, but what is required now is the epistemological order. We must begin with what we know.

37

There are many points in a reasonable faith which, however important they may be, are not starting points. Conspicuous among these is belief in life after death. Though there are excellent reasons for believing that conscious life after death is not a mere speculation, the conclusions are all derivative; they depend upon other items of a reasonable faith. The life everlasting is soundly based if it is seen as a corollary, but it is almost meaningless if it stands alone. In a different way, belief in God is not a good place to start, because of the intrinsic ambiguity involved. God can mean almost anything, and has in fact meant widely different things to different believers. The idea of God can be either the noblest idea the human mind can entertain, or something so vague that it is hardly a subject of rational discourse.

We require a place to start which is both concrete and meaningful. Recognizing the fallibility of the human mind, we do not expect, as did Descartes, to find something "indubitable" to begin with, but we do have a right to look for something which has reasonable stability. Modern man, we all realize, is Cartesian in that he carries on a dramatic dialogue within himself, doubting in order to know. The way of wisdom is to construct our faith on what we have the most reason to trust, for groundless trust is indistinguishable from superstition.

A Christian is a person who, with all the honesty of which he is capable, becomes convinced that the fact of Jesus Christ is the most trustworthy that he knows in his entire universe of discourse. Christ thus becomes both his central postulate and the Archimedean fulcrum which, because it is really firm, enables him to operate with confidence in other areas. Few in our generation have said this as succinctly as has Charles Davis, until recently the leading Roman Catholic theologian of Great Britain. Because Davis found that he had ample reason to doubt some of the dogmas of his particular church, he sorrowfully left it, but he did not thereby cease to be a Christian. Indeed, his intellectual struggle made his central conviction about Christ all the more firm. In a brief but memorable sentence this honest thinker has said, "Faith is a personal commitment to Jesus Christ."[1]

For the Christian, Christ is not the end of the quest; He is the beginning. Starting with Him, we are forced by intellectual integrity to proceed a long way. If we are committed to Him, we trust Him about the being and the character of God, about the reality of prayer, about the possibility of miracle, and about the life everlasting. The deepest conviction of the Christian is that Christ was not wrong! Particularly, we are convinced that He was not wrong in His report about Himself. It is important to remember that our commitment is to one who said, "All things have been delivered to me by my Father; and no one knows the Son except the Father, and no one knows the Father except the Son and any one to whom the Son chooses to reveal him" (Matt. 11:27).

To say that Christ is the fulcrum is not merely to say that He was the greatest figure of history or the finest moral teacher. It is, instead, to see Him as the genuine revelation of the mystery of existence, the one clear light among the many shadows. Commitment is thus vastly more than mere admiration. It means passionate involvement in His life, teachings, death, and resurrection. It is to share with Him when He says, "I am the resurrection and the life" (John 11:25). We are not Christians until we are committed, and we are not committed until we combine, in our faith in Christ, the reasons of the heart with the

---

1 Charles Davis, *A Question of Conscience* (New York: Harper & Row, 1967), p. 181.

reasons of the intellect. Commitment to Christ does not solve our problems; on the contrary, it adds new ones. Often it brings not peace but a sword (Matt. 10:34), because it produces a holy disturbance. In any case, it destroys what is ordinarily understood as peace of mind. Like Archimedes, we still have to do the work of lifting, but we have a solid point from which to operate.

One way in which freshness may be achieved in the contemporary situation is by helping people to ask new questions. To many the question of the divinity of Christ seems stale and boring, but often these same people can become genuinely interested when they are involved in a radically different approach. This different approach, which stresses the Christlikeness of God, has an immense intellectual appeal because it enables men to move from the relatively known to the relatively unknown, the freshness of the approach lying as much as in the question as in the answer. The question becomes, "What is God like?" Is God a mere impersonal force? Is God merely a Ground of Being? Is God vindictive and uncaring? Or is God like Jesus Christ? Jesus Himself answers this last question in the affirmative, and if it is a true answer it is the most exciting news in all the world. A Christian, however imperfect he may be, is a believer, and *this* is what he believes.

One of the most striking advantages of beginning with Christ rather than with God is that this method brings together people who are far apart in other matters of belief. Even Bishop John Robinson, when he wrote *Honest to God*, was certainly no friend of theism, yet stressed commitment to Christ and quoted approvingly the now familiar words of Professor Butterfield, "Hold to Christ, and for the rest be totally uncommitted."[2] And Professor Altizer, though

2 Herbert Butterfield, *Christianity and History* (New York: Charles Scribner's Sons, 1950), p. 146.

an explicit atheist, finds in Christ his solid point. In short, though it may not be possible for theologians to unite on the being and nature of God, there is a practical basis of unity in Christian commitment. However great the confusion may be, it is wise to be thankful for something in common. Though the common ground has not yet led to agreement about its implications, the intelligible procedure is to start from such a position and to proceed in the unremitting effort to see where it leads.

Before we look carefully at the implications of the Christian fulcrum, however, we must face the insistent question of why the fulcrum is accepted. Why hold to Christ? What is there about Him which convinces us that He provides the one firm ground mortal men can know? This question has always been asked, but because of widespread interest in, and some knowledge of, world religions it is being asked with renewed insistence today. Admitting that He made extreme claims, what reason (we ask ourselves in our insistent dialogue) is there to suppose that Christ's claims have any justification?

It is popular in some circles to accept Christ as a teacher, but not as one who provides a unique revelation of the Father. The familiar stance is one that involves admiring comments about Christ but denies any supernaturalism. Such a position, however, cannot be defended rationally, since all four Gospels bristle with supernatural claims on the part of Jesus. The person who takes this position has surely not read the Gospels! Familiarity has blinded men to the radical nature of Christ's claims about His peculiar relationship to the Father. Both C. S. Lewis and J. B. Phillips have performed a useful service in helping readers to see that the only alternative to acceptance of Christ's teaching about Himself is that He was either "a lunatic or a quack." "Now if He believed thus and spoke thus," writes Phillips, "and failed to rise from the dead, He was, without question, a lunatic. He was quite plainly a young idealist suffering from *folie de grandeur* on the biggest possible scale, and cannot on that account be regarded as the World's Greatest Teacher."[3] *The inescapable conclusion is that, if Christ was only a teacher, He was a very misleading teacher.*

To give all the reasons for accepting Christ as our fulcrum would take a long time and is perhaps impossible, but enough can be said briefly to indicate the logic of such belief. Though in any system, whether mathematical or scientific, the ultimate postulates are beyond absolute proof, this does not mean that they are arbitrarily adopted. The conviction that Christ makes more sense than does anything else we know rests, not upon a single line of evidence, but upon a combination of many different factors which, together, give cumulatively the power of convincement. Once it was common to say that the Christian revelation carries its own authority,[4] and this may be true, but the assertion is seldom convincing to contemporary man. Modern man asks, and rightly, for more reasons. Certainly we need something better than mere tradition. It is not sufficient to say "Believe!" for then we fall back into the heresy of fideism. It is not adequate to say, "My mother taught me," for mothers teach a great variety of beliefs, some of which are clearly false.

When Blaise Pascal tried to explain why he was convinced that Christ is the place to stand, he referred to "Jesus Christ, whom the Testaments regard, the old as its hope, the new its model, and both as their center."[5] The very system of dating which makes Christ the dividing point in history is a largely unconscious recognition of what Pascal

---

[3] J. B. Phillips, *Your God Is Too Small* (New York: The MacMillan Co., 1967), p. 113.
[4] See Edwin Lewis, *The Faith We Declare* (Nashville, Tenn: Cokesbury Press, 1939), p. 15.
[5] *Pensées*, No. 739.

explicitly recognized. Because we can easily see that persons are the most important realities in the universe as it is known to us, we center the historical process in a person—but which one? To date all documents from Julius Caesar would be ridiculous, because that would overglorify the patently local, but about Christ there is an obvious universality. We can be grateful for the rationality of *Anno Domini*. All our dating, whether B.C. or A.D., is a tacit acknowledgment that a significant fact about any other event in history is whether it happened before or after His coming. Tiberius and Herod lived when He lived, but nobody would be foolish enough to date from them.

The most pragmatic of reasons for seeing that Christ is the most dependable of realities is that of changed human lives. When we consider Saul of Tarsus on the road to Damascus, we are in the realm of the empirical as contrasted with the merely speculative. Saul said it was the Living Christ who had met him, and the person who seeks to deny this is confronted with the fact of a permanent change in Saul's character. We cannot, of course, know whether a man is lying when he says "I believe," because belief is intrinsically internal and personal, but the evidence of changed lives is something which other people can observe. In Saul's case the change was so radical that it led to the production of some of the finest literature of the world, a literature which would not have been produced apart from the crucial encounter.

The evidence of lives changed by contact with Christ is so abundant that the full story can never be told; it is, indeed, of a kind not matched anywhere in any culture. The changed lives have come about, not primarily by a set of ideas or by acceptance of a doctrine, but by commitment to a Person. Long after the time of the Apostle Paul a man named Francis, who lived in Assisi, exhibited a change so great that he in turn mightily affected others. G. K. Chesterton has told us how this came about. "A man," he says, "will not roll in the snow for a stream of tendency by which all things fulfill the law of their being. He will not go without food in the name of something, not ourselves, that makes for righteousness. He will do things like this, or pretty nearly like this, under quite a different impulse. He will do these things when he is in love."[6]

The Christian takes his stand on the fact that lives can be made new by fellowship with Christ, and he does not know of any other source of change and renewal which is equal to this. With George Fox, the Christian of each generation hears an inner voice which says, "There is one, even Christ Jesus, who can speak to thy condition."[7] We have learned that a mere inner direction, no matter how frantic or obsessive, is not sufficient for the new life we sorely need, for we do not have the power to save ourselves. My own life cannot be unified except by that to which I am devoted. But where shall I turn? A mere "ism" will never suffice. Because persons are superior, in kind, not only to all *things* but even to all *ideas,* I need a person to whom I can give myself and thereby find myself. But not just any person will suffice; it must be a person commitment to whom can change the imperfect world order.

We may consider turning to Karl Marx, but his is not a sufficiently revolutionary mentality. Because we are dulled by familiarity we forget, sometimes, that Christ provides the most revolutionary of conceptions, in that He sees each individual as an unconditional object of the divine Concern. This undermines all racism and, when taken seriously, provides an antidote to all injustice. The radical solution

---

6 G. K. Chesterton, *St. Francis of Assisi* (New York: George H. Doran Co., 1924) , p. 20.

7 *Journal of George Fox* (Cambridge, Eng.: The University Press, 1952) , p. 11.

of the race question rests ultimately upon the recognition, as Carl Henry says, that "the Negro is not only politically an equal but spiritually a brother."[8] And so is each one, whoever he is! The Fatherly care, says Christ, extends to each object of His creation, including the sparrow, whose fall to the ground is a matter of importance. But of even more significance is what transpires in the life of any finite person who is made in God's image. "You," said Christ, "are of more value than many sparrows" (Matt. 10:31).

It cannot be too strongly asserted that one of the chief reasons for seeing that commitment to Christ makes sense is recognition of the social effects of such commitment, for what has been termed the social gospel is merely the reasonable application of the total gospel. It is no accident that the real pioneering in recognition of the sinfulness of human slavery came from men whose lives were centered on Christ in the most absolute way. It is time to make clear that the assumption of a necessary conflict between an evangelical faith and a bold social witness is completely false. More than one historical scholar has pointed out, for example, that the Trade Union movement in England derives more from John Wesley than from Karl Marx. The strongest leaders of the English antislavery movement were unashamed evangelicals. The truth is that the more a man centers on the love of Christ, the more he is constrained to work for justice among his fellow men. There are many reasons for this consequence, one of them being that the Christ-centered man listens to One who said, "As you did it to one of the least of these my my brethren, you did it to me" (Matt. 25:40). The thoughtful person who asks seriously, "To whom else shall we go?" encounters great difficulty in imagining any other center

[8] Carl F. H. Henry, *The God Who Shows Himself* (Waco, Tex.: Word Books, 1966), p. 71.

of commitment which can provide a more powerful motive for changing the world.

There is no doubt that many of our contemporaries are devoted to the pursuit of scientific research in a manner that makes them selfless. Though for this we ought to be humbly grateful, there is no reason to suppose that commitment to science is equal to commitment to Christ. After all, science is an abstraction, while Christ is a concrete Person. I can love science, but science cannot love me. Furthermore, the love of Christ, far from being incompatible with scientific excellence, can make a man an even better scientist.[9] The more he centers on Christ, the more he seeks to love God *with all his mind*. In addition, he has an added reason to maintain an affectionate relationship with his fellow scientists.

When we have mentioned the revolutionary mentality and the scientific mentality, we have very little left in the way of live alternatives to Christ as the Ground of Trustworthiness. There are, of course, those who adopt what they call a Playboy Philosophy, but this does not include any revolutionary passion. Relativism sounds good to many, especially when they receive a little education and learn, essentially for the first time, that there are many different human cultures; but relativism is not, and cannot be, a mature philosophical position. It has never recovered from the examination administered by Socrates, as reported by Plato in the *Theaetetus*. The position of the Sophists is certainly no more defensible in the twentieth century than it was in the fifth century B.C., when Socrates analyzed it with such damaging effect.

On January 14, 1968, a remarkable chapter was enacted

[9] One good illustration is seen in the work of C. A. Coulson, Rouse Ball Professor of Mathematics at Oxford University. Professor Coulson, who is both a Methodist lay preacher and director of the Mathematical Institute at Oxford, finds the combination helpful.

in the intellectual life of our generation. The occasion was the rectorial address of Malcolm Muggeridge at the University of Edinburgh. The famous satirist, one-time editor of *Punch,* alluded to the shoddy and sentimental outlooks which have had to do duty in an age when more profound beliefs have been in abeyance. "We all know," he said, "how increasingly hollow and unconvincing it is—the great society, mankind coming of age, men like gods, all the unspeakable cant of Utopians on the run." The brilliant humorist was deadly serious, thus reminding us of the remark of Socrates at the end of the *Symposium,* that the genius of comedy is the same as that of tragedy, and that the true artist in one may also be an artist in the other.

Muggeridge, at St. Giles in Edinburgh, was using his sharp wit to puncture the pretensions of many systems which have been taken overseriously in our time. He knows that the talk of mankind come of age is sheer cant; we are actually closer to the kindergarten. He knows how silly it is to speak of the human situation as being radically new. There are no new sins and there are no new virtues. He knows that the Great Society simply does not come to pass. We have not overcome poverty and we have not prevented lawlessness, to say nothing of war. However desperate the case for theism may be, the case for humanism is a far more desperate one. Sun worship, however pagan, might be a more wholesome thing than man's worship of himself. Largely because the known alternatives will not suffice, Muggeridge turns to Christ as the one rational hope, for the shoddiness of the idols leaves room for the real. The satirist's conclusion, which he had the courage to state before an audience of contemporary students, was: "As far as I am concerned, it is Christ or nothing." Atheism would not have been shocking at all, for it would have been merely conventional, but it was intensely shocking for the rector to make an unapologetically evangelical witness, and to give the reasons why. His major conclusion was:

> So I come back to where I began, to the other king, one Jesus, to the Christian notion that man's efforts to make himself personally and collectively happy in earthly terms are doomed to failure. He must, indeed, as Christ said, be born again, be a new man, or he's nothing. So at least I have concluded, having failed to find in past experience, present dilemmas and future expectations, any alternative proposition.[10]

A man of the mentality of Muggeridge is, of course, not opposed to ideas, since ideas are his stock in trade. But he knows with George Eliot that "ideas are poor ghosts until they become incarnate in a person." What we find in Christ, as nowhere else in the whole world, is the perfect combination of words and deeds. Though it is the sad lot of human kind to move back and forth between utopianism and despair, Christ consistently avoids both these opposite errors. While recognizing a potential ground of hope in any person, including a prostitute or a criminal like the thief on the cross, He avoids the sentimental idea of natural human goodness. He knows that the worker for justice may himself be corruptible, and that those who do not love money may, nevertheless, love power over others. Indeed, His indictment of religious leaders makes harsh reading. One of the most profound of the recorded remarks of Christ appears in the Sermon on the Mount when He says, "If, then, the light in you is darkness, how great is the darkness!" (Matt. 6:23). What if the colleges, which are organized for the sake of cure, become themselves, evidences of the disease? What if religious leaders demonstrate what they are supposed to overcome? In short, deep corruption is possible, and it is possible at any human

10 Malcolm Muggeridge, *Another King* (Edinburgh: St. Andrews Press, 1968), pp.12, 13.

level. The Christian faith, whatever else it may be, is not sentimental; it does not speak of the inevitability of progress or of "men like gods." Whenever it is loyal to Christ it stresses both elements in the paradox of the nobility and degradation of mankind. Humor is one method by which the paradox may be presented, and this is especially true when the humor serves to reduce human pretensions to their normal size. We are no longer surprised at the hatred which contemporary leaders felt for Christ when we consider that he made them appear laughable. Only a person who has been brainwashed into overseriousness can fail to smile at the spectacle of holy men who strain out tiny insects while they swallow camels, humps and all (Matt. 23:24).

It is hard to imagine the effect on a mature mind of coming in contact for the first time with the Beatitudes. Our common trouble is that we have heard these words so long that we mistakenly suppose we comprehend them. Is it true that the meek inherit the earth? Most people do not think so. But what if "meek" means "harnessed"? What if Christ means that the final effectiveness comes through humble-minded persons who have transcended the cult of empty freedom by finding One to whom they are fully committed? Then we see the linguistic connection between the third Beatitude and the Yoke passage (Matt. 11:28–30), and realize that the call "Come to me," the clearest call to commitment Christ is known to have made, involves a new level of freedom to those who are yoked with Him. Utopia we do not expect, because of human finitude and chronic self-centeredness, but we do know, from experience, that those who achieve this kind of meekness are the ones who make the world relatively better. The eighteenth-century New Jersey tailor John Woolman provides a superb example of this "bold meekness." Woolman

was bold in social pioneering, especially in recognizing slavery
as a sin, but he never forgot the One to whom his life
and mind were committed. When he spoke for the last
time, just before dying of smallpox in 1772, he said, "I
believe my being here is in the wisdom of Christ."[11] The
meek may not seem to inherit the earth, but they certainly
change it!

The profundity of Christ's recorded thought has led to the
use of the expression "the mind of Christ." Certainly we do
not know all that was, or is, in His mind, and there is no
reason to suppose that the recorded utterances of the four
Gospels give more than a mere fraction of what He said; but
we know something. The crucial passage is stated in characteristic paradox when Paul quotes Isaiah 40:13, "For who has
known the mind of the Lord so as to instruct him?" and then
adds "But we have the mind of Christ" (I Cor. 2:16).

The Christian who uses the phrase "the mind of Christ" is
not using language in the same way as if he were to speak of
the mind of Plato or Marx. We know something of the minds
of these men because we can read what they wrote, but we
mean something different in reference to Christ. We mean
that Christ can be in *us,* that His very mentality comes to
dominate ours. "Do you not realize," asks Paul, "that Jesus
Christ is in you?" (II Cor. 13:5). Shocking as it sounds, it is
really possible for a finite man, as he responds to Christ's call
to have a measure of the spirit of Christ. The central purpose
of the gospel is that Christ may be formed in *us* (Gal. 4:19)
and that He may dwell in our hearts (Eph. 3:17).

As the Apostle Paul saw, in the striking paradox based
upon his acquaintance with the Hebrew Scriptures, no finite
individual can fully know God, for God is both invisible and
largely inscrutable; but that is not the end of the story. In

11 *The Journal of John Woolman* (New York: The Macmillan Co., 1922),
p. 325.

Christ we have something gloriously concrete, "the image of the invisible God" (Col. 1:15). Though we cannot know all of Christ's thoughts, we know some, and we can verify in a measure His affirmation that further revelation of His mind merely awaits our ability to listen (John 16:12).

We speak only with tremendous reticence about the "mind of God," but we can speak with some confidence about the mind of Christ. Never should we cease to be thankful for the production and preservation of the four Gospels. In spite of the welcome scientific study of historical and literary origins, they stand up remarkably under full and sustained examination. Though New Testament scholarship has made great advances, there is no good reason why the ordinary Christian should be intimidated by the confident assertions of men who claim to know definitely which parts of the Gospel record are original and which were added as a result of the needs and experience of the early Church. The person who claims to be able to say, with certitude, which of the Gospel passages are authentic utterances of Christ and which are not, is claiming more than any man actually knows. In this connection we can be helped by C. S. Lewis when he says, "Don't let us be too easily brow-beaten."[12] It is important to remember that the new knowledge of the flesh-and-blood Christ is something we owe to the Church. It is not true, therefore, as is sometimes said, that the early Church was interested only in the Eternal or risen Lord. There is little doubt that the chief incentive for the production of accounts of what Christ did and said and suffered was that early Christians, many of whom were Greek, desired to know the objective and historical truth about His appearing. The Gospels were the response of those who knew.

The early Christian desire for the production of Gospels is

12 *Letters to Malcolm: Chiefly on Prayer* (New York: Harcourt, Brace & World, 1963), p. 36.

an important revelation. The members of the early Church wanted to know more about Christ because they believed that He was the image of God the Father. They could find out very little by any direct means of encounter with God, but they believed that they could learn a great deal by encountering Him indirectly, through Christ. Their tremendous affirmation, which underlies all they did and said and which is the secret of their boldness, was that though they could not see God they could see His *image*, and they wanted to learn more about that image. It was because they believed that Christ was more than Teacher that they wanted to know the details of His teaching. Early Christians preserved the record of the teachings of Christ because they were convinced that He was not merely a teacher. Only on this hypothesis can we account for the fact that they went to so much trouble. They took great pains to know Christ because, facing the facts of His life, they had concluded that he was indeed the very brightness of God's own glory and "the express image of God's person" (Heb. 1:3, A.V.) .

Though it was once fashionable to make a sharp distinction between the historic Christ and the Living Christ, it is no longer so. What we see is that this sharp distinction cannot be meaningfully made, because in both cases we are dealing with the same reality. Since Christ can be our Teacher as truly today as He was the Teacher of the apostles by the Sea of Galilee, it is blasphemous to speak of Him merely in the past tense. Tremendous excitement is involved in the idea that Christ can be known in the present tense, and that He can be known in the most mundane events. When we speak of the Living Christ we do not mean the same as when we refer to the "spirit of Abraham Lincoln," which is another matter altogether. We mean, in reference to the Living Christ; that Christ is a Person who is still alive in very fact, and not metaphorically. Only the naïve would suppose that this living reality is a matter of flesh. But what good reason is there, after all, to suppose that fleshly existence is the only form of existence?

When we speak of the Living Christ we do not refer to the reserved sacrament. Christ, as we know Him now, is not something which can be carried about in a box and adored. The Real Presence is never confined to an altar, and indeed has no connection with any magic at all. The doctrine of the real presence is simply a way of affirming the fact that humble men and women who are neither insane nor stupid find that He is with them on life's darkest as well as its brightest ways. Because Christ is alive, He is not limited to one area or one historic period. Though He was in Galilee, He is not confined to Galilee. Fortunately, neither is He confined to the West, nor identified with it.

One of the finest fruits of the Christian revelation is the way in which it makes world religions allies rather than competitors. Christ came, He said, not to destroy but to fulfill. Anything valuable in Buddhism or Hinduism or Islam we can therefore honor and employ, for Christ has "other sheep, that are not of this fold" (John 10:16). The spirit of this important insight is caught in the prologue of the Letter to the Hebrews, "In many and various ways God spoke of old." All the insights of the Hebrew prophets are ennobled by the new context which Christ provides. The effect of this on missionary work is crucial, for the wise missionary, rather than being the servant or exponent of Western civilazation, is instead the messenger of Christ. Although, if he is a mature thinker, he knows that the redemptive fellowship is important, he does not feel it necessary to defend the Church. Instead of being the servant of Christianity, he is an apostle of Christ. This is possible because Christ, far from being an item of our culture, belongs in reality to all cultures, and is the Judge of all, including our own.

When we try seriously to be faithful to the Biblical message in its wholeness, we are careful not to claim too much. The powerful influence of Karl Barth has made some believe that knowledge of God is limited to the Christian revelation as found in the Bible, but this is unbiblical. The Barthian error, of course, is not Barth's insistence on the centrality of Christ, but his virtual denial of the idea that in pre-Christian ages God "did not leave himself without witness" (Acts 14:17). Though the revelation in nature is manifestly incomplete, it is nevertheless real, and a man can have *some* knowledge even before he meets Jesus Christ. John Baillie took great pains to make this clear in the Gifford Lectures which he wrote but never delivered.

I had, of course [he says], always believed that there is no ultimate salvation for mankind save in Jesus Christ, but when I began to read Dr. Barth's books, what struck me at once as unfamiliar was his insistence that mankind had no *knowledge* of God save in Jesus Christ. This is new teaching and it is precisely what I have never been able to accept.[13]

We sometimes speak of the present time as the post-Christian age, and this language is accurate providing it is understood. It must not mean that Christ has been either transcended or outmoded, for even those who give Him no conscious thought are deeply influenced by Him to this day. Whatever we do, we cannot be as though Christ had never spoken, for He troubles our otherwise easy consciences. The old pre-Christian standard of values exemplified and promulgated by some of the Caesars cannot be accepted again, for Christ planted in all men a radically new idea: that the central mark of greatness is service (Luke 22:25–27). The distinguished Jewish scholar, Dr. Claude Montefiore, has held that Christ brought into the world something which even the

---

[13] John Baillie, *The Sense of the Presence of God* (New York: Charles Scribner's Sons, 1962), p. 255.

rabbinical literature did not envisage, when He elevated the ideal of service. Humility had indeed been mentioned, but the combination of humility and service, illustrated by the washing of the feet of the disciples, was novel. Even though we give Him little attention, Christ has added to our predicament; He has made it impossible to be easily satisfied with the mere lust for power. After nearly two thousand years, He is still the Great Disturber. To this day it is difficult to read His words and still be satisfied with one's own life.

We tend to proceed with a spiritual naïveté, unaware of the sources of our convictions. When we extol service as the mark of greatness, we honor a humility which is more noble than pride, but seldom realize that we might not have understood any of these things apart from Christ. Certainly we did not discover them by ourselves. Without Him, we should not have understood that it is these very ideas that provide us with some understanding of the Maker of heaven and earth. What if the Eternal Mind, underlying all reality, were indeed the Suffering Servant, with the spirit of the little child? The astounding relevation is that this is true!

How do we know that it is true? Speculation and abstract reasoning do not carry us far. This is why it is rational to talk of Christ before we talk of God. But the odd consequence is that, when we talk of Christ, almost our only intellectual resource is a story. The Christian, when challenged, merely tells the story again, because that is all that there is to do. The story asserts that once, during the days when the Roman Empire was powerful, there was One who lived in such a manner that those who knew Him best became convinced that His life represented a unique revelation of the Living God. In harmony with what He said of Himself, they concluded that, since He could not be accounted for by ordinary canons of judgment, He represented a divine breakthrough into history. This One was no imperial Caesar, no hero of

romance, no respected philosopher. He spent His youth in a
carpenter's shop; He lived His days in the greatest possible
simplicity; He forgathered with the sick rather than with
those who were whole; He was the instrument of healing for
many who suffered from physical diseases as well as those
whose troubles were primarily spiritual. He unabashedly
claimed to present accurately and authentically the "Character of God."[14]

He unhesitatingly announced the forgiveness of sins, a fact
which was of great importance in that He moved more
among sinners than among righteous men. His career was
marked by self-spending rather than self-saving and this continued through His death, which was that of a public criminal. After death He appeared in both a bodily and a spiritual
manner to a great many people whose lives were consequently revolutionized. There are many who affirm that the
story is not yet finished, because He meets with them *now*.

We have a tendency, of course, to say the words of a creed
mindlessly, but the most familiar words would shake us if we
were to understand them. The worshiper who says, "I believe
in Jesus Christ," is really saying that the story termed the
Incarnation presents the truth as abstraction can never do.
To believe in Christ is to believe that God is like Him, and
that is to believe that suffering love rather than sheer power
stands at the center of all reality. To believe in Christ is to be
convinced that suffering and long-suffering love constitute
the very pillars upon which the universe is built. Important
as thinking is, the deepest truth appears not in ideas but in
events.

Since there is really no other one to whom to turn, the
only alternative for one who will not accept Christ as the
fulcrum is to have no fulcrum, but in that direction lies con-

---

14 See in this connection J. B. Phillips, *Your God is Too Small, op. cit.*,
p. 85.

tinued confusion. If life does not have a center, it cannot even have a periphery. The Christian has no means of convincing others concerning the solid point of the universe except that of first asking his neighbor really to look at the story, and, second, demonstrating in his own life the power and compassion that come by operating from this solid point. Because there is no possibility of effective argument apart from experience, the sole practical method is that of looking. "Only look!" we must say. "Look, first, at what Christ did in His life on earth, and look again at what He has done among men in subsequent generations!"

In an age when the claims of Christ are widely disputed, or what is worse, neglected, the committed Christian must re-examine his entire strategy, for acceptance cannot be assumed. All that remains is witness; but this is, after all, the most convincing approach. Even in the darkest time the Christian affirms, humbly yet unapologetically, that Christ has reached Him and that, though he is still imperfect, there is a profound sense in which his life has been made new. Herein lies the powerful answer of John Baillie, to whom modern Christians are so deeply indebted.

I do know that in fact it is the constraint of Jesus Christ from which I find it most impossible to escape. I just cannot read the Gospel story without knowing that I am being sought out in love, that I am at the same time being called to life's most sacred task and being offered life's highest prize. For it is the love God has shown me in Christ that constrains me to the love of my fellow men. If there be someone who is aware of no such constraint, I cannot, of course, hope to make him aware of it by speaking these few sentences. That would require, not so much a more elaborate argument as something quite different from any argument. But I am not now arguing. I am only confessing.[15]

15 John Baillie, *A Reasoned Faith* (New York: Charles Scribner's Sons, 1963) , pp. 118, 119.

When any sincere seeker asks seriously, without being captious, why Christ is chosen as a firm alternative to confusion, the plain answer is to challenge him to try the experiment. Most of those who reject Christ do so from ignorance, for they have not really faced Him. Anyone who believes in the experimental method, and who is sufficiently aware of human failure to know that some answer is needed, may reasonably be expected to respond to such a challenge. But without these conditions, nothing of importance will occur. Pascal's defense of the Christian faith is a powerful one, but he well understood that neither his nor any other approach could make headway with those who were afraid to be open-minded about Christ. "Men despise religion," he said. "They hate it and fear it is true."[16]

The practical advice, then, is to adopt the experimental method. Live with the Gospels every day for a solid year, reading short consecutive passages, marking, questioning, and if possible praying. This is a dangerous experiment, for it may change your life. As Schweitzer taught us long ago, you need not start with any preconceived judgment of who He is. Christ's first followers, as Schweitzer observed, were drawn to Him before they knew who He was.[17] The same can happen to us today. Perhaps, after much confrontation, the answer will come to us as it came to them.

16 *Pensées*, No. 187.
17 Albert Schweitzer, *The Quest of the Historical Jesus* (New York: The MacMillan Co., 1922) , p. 401.

CHAPTER III

THE LIVING GOD

In addition to all finite selves there is a being called God, numerically distinct from them, an independent centre of consciousness, with his own unique life and purposes, with a differential activity of his own.

—CHARLES A. BENNETT

If Christ is trustworthy, God really is! I have many reasons for believing in God, but the one reason which I find inescapable is the testimony of Christ. Having made Him my center of certitude, it is not rational to refuse to follow Him in His own deepest experience and conviction. "Testimony," as Dr. Johnson observed, "has great weight, and casts the balance."[1]

The testimony of Christ is important because thoughtful people are fully aware of a certain inconclusiveness in all other theistic evidences. There are evidences that God is and there are evidences which, taken alone, indicate that God is not. The employment of testimony, and especially that of Christ, is an effort to use all the intelligence we have in the greatest matters, as we try to do in matters of less intrinsic importance. No man knows definitely how the planets were formed, but it makes sense to take seriously the conclusions of

[1] Boswell, *Life of Samuel Johnson, op. cit.,* Vol. I, p. 318.

the most eminent astronomers. When we cannot know alone, the logical procedure is to trust those who have already shown themselves trustworthy.

Even when we pursue the method of comparative difficulties, as described in Chapter I, we soon realize that we need something more in order to justify a conclusion. Here, as in so many other areas of thought, Pascal provides us with a fruitful suggestion. "Let us examine this point, and say 'God is, or He is not.' But to which side shall we incline?"[2] Since our experience is finite, there is no absolute and incontrovertible proof either way. The uncertainty, of course, is not in the objective fact, but in *us*. Why not, then, forget it or refuse to decide? Because, says Pascal, "It is not optional. You are embarked." The man who says that he will not decide whether to let the weeds of his garden go to seed is really deluding himself, for he has already decided. Indecision, in crucial matters, is itself a decision! It is at this point that Pascal introduces the famous conception of the wager. At the deepest points of his life it is required of a man that he be a gambler, and in our greatest gamble it is reasonable to allow the testimony of Christ to tip the balance. *A Christian is one who bets his life that Christ is right.*

Though the characteristic modern man is confused at many points, he is especially confused about the being of God, but this is not primarily on account of old-fashioned atheism, which has been with us for a long time. There is a certain grandeur about the classic and utterly undisguised atheism, especially when it is expressed in the moving rhetoric of Lord Russell. Personally, I am glad to report the nobility I sensed in Russell's central statement when I first read it more than forty years ago.

That Man is the product of causes which had no prevision of the end they were achieving; that his origin, his growth, his hopes

2 *Pensées,* No. 233

and fears, his loves and his beliefs, are but the outcome of accidental collocations of atoms; that no fire, no heroism, no intensity of thought and feeling, can preserve an individual life beyond the grave; that all the labours of the ages, all the devotion, all the inspiration, all the noonday brightness of human genius, are destined to extinction in the vast death of the solar system, and that the whole temple of Man's achievement must inevitably be buried beneath the débris of a universe in ruins—all these things, if not quite beyond dispute, and are yet so nearly certain, that no philosophy which rejects them can hope to stand.[3]

After sixty-five years, the British philosopher has not renounced this position.

A man who is a sincere atheist may be a personally good man, and usually he is not stupid. He may be an honest thinker who has come reluctantly and sadly to the conclusion that, though there are some reasons for believing that man is not alone in his struggles for decency and order, there are more compelling reasons for concluding that he *is* alone. Such a conclusion will not make an intelligent person happy, but that, for an honest thinker, is never the primary consideration. The Christian should be the first to honor honest doubt, partly because he experiences so much of it in his own internal dialogue. Like the atheist, he is worried by the problem of how, if God is, there is so much unmerited suffering in the world. He knows that this is a problem which we never wholly solve, even though we do so in part, but he also knows that it is unphilosophical to determine any question of importance by one objection alone.

The major alternative to atheism such as that expressed by Bertrand Russell is called "theism." By this is meant the conviction, eloquently expressed by the late Professor Bennett[4] of

[3] Bertrand Russell, *Mysticism and Logic* (Garden City, N.Y.: Doubleday Anchor Books, 1957), p. 45.

[4] After his death, Professor Bennett's widow made available to me his unpublished papers. Thus I owe to him many ideas which he never published.

Yale, in the epigraph that introduces this particular chapter. A theist is one who believes that in addition to the physical universe, and also in additiom to human beings, such as ourselves, there is One who gives meaning to all existence. The theist believes that God *was* before the world was created, and that He still *will be,* even if our physical universe runs down or is rolled up like a scroll (Isa. 34:4). In the theistic conception God is not only the Creator, without whom the world as we know it would not be, but also the One who is constantly sustaining the world order and is involved in every step. The order of nature, far from limiting God's action in the present world, is dependent upon His purpose and subservient to it. The order is dependable, not because it is mechanical or unchangeable, but because it is purposive and therefore intelligent.

According to theism, God is completely and radically personal. By this theists mean that God is not a mere Ground of Being but One to whom personal pronouns can be applied with intellectual honesty. He is not an "it," or an abstraction. Above all, says the theist, God is the One with whom it is possible for even finite men to have an "I-Thou" relationship. He is One who can be encountered in prayer as well as the providential guidance of our lives. Every finite person is an object of His infinite care, known and loved individually. This is the conception of God that underlies, at every point, the Hebrew and Christian Scriptures which we call the Bible. It is the conception that dominates the recorded life and teachings of Christ, for in Christ Biblical theism reaches its climax and fulfillment.

The new developments in the contemporary scene which have produced so much erosion of faith differ radically from the ancient denial of God which men expect and know how to handle. Confusion arises because there are many widely publicized systems of thought which use some theistic language, and even speak of prayer, yet in which the words when carefully examined turn out to mean something different. Some authors spread confusion by quoting the Bible while at the same time rejecting the central conception of God that Christ reveals.

It is important to understand that what is popularly termed "Christian atheism" is not a serious threat. This is because the self-contradication is obvious. The Christian atheist is one who claims to be committed to Christ but does not believe that God, the Creator and Sustainer of the world, *is*. The oddity of this position lies in the joint effort to believe in Christ and yet not to accept Christ's own central conviction. Since there is a manifest absurdity in trusting Christ and yet rejecting the implications of that position, it would be intellectually more respectable to say openly that Christ was wrong. This particular development may be accurately called Unitarianism of the Second Person, since it has nothing to say of God the Father or of the Holy Spirit. At Amsterdam twenty years ago I heard a speaker say, "All I care about is Jesus Christ." Though the speaker was Christ-centered, he was confusedly so, for it is a mark of clarity never to accept a position unless one is willing to accept what that position entails. "If you knew me," said Christ, "you would know my Father also" (John 8:19).

The thoughtful adherent of Basic Christianity, who takes Christ as his fulcrum and accepts what this involves, need not be greatly worried about the movement just mentioned. It is espoused by only a tiny minority; it has at this time no standing in any theological seminary; and it will soon be forgotten. The theistic faith is an anvil which has worn out many hammers, and it will wear out this one. If some popular writers make it hard to believe in God, this is not the worst that can occur, for belief in God ought not to be made easy. It is never true that the existence of God is simple and obvious! The man who says that he needs only to look at a flower to know that God exists is not really helping anybody, not even himself, for though the flower is undoubtedly beautiful there is likewise much in our world that is ugly and cruel. Easy faith is almost as damaging as is the easy conscience.

Far more important than "Christian atheism" is a position which has a variety of exponents with the uniting feature that it attempts to present an alternative to both atheism and theism. The various strands of such a position have been known to theological scholars for several decades, but the central idea received its present notoriety when, in 1963, an Anglican clergyman, the Bishop of Woolwich, wrote a small book called *Honest to God*. The spectacle of a Christian spokesman espousing a position critical of theism, yet speaking reverently of God, attracted readers by the hundreds of thousands. The book is important now only because it was the means by which a multitude of readers became aware of what was going on. Though there are some who have been helped by this book, and who even report that Bishop Robinson has given them a faith by which they can live, there are others, probably the majority, who report that the discussion has eroded much of the faith they once had. What is required, therefore, is a concerted effort to cut through the fog that is baffling so many sincere minds. The right start in this undertaking is to make distinctions between the strands of thought in what is popularly called the New Theology.

The theology which is most mystifying to the contemporary Christian has three important marks. In general its conception of God is:

1. Anti-existent.
2. Antisupernatural.
3. Antipersonal.

Puzzling as these negations may seem, and curious as it is that they can be held by people who believe in God, they are not really as difficult as they appear. There is a reason for each conception, and it is a reason which can be understood, providing we are willing to engage in the ministry of clarity.

First let us consider existence. Though most professing Christians have never read the major works of the late Paul Tillich, many have heard his name and have a vague idea that this eminent theologian denied the existence of God, and furthermore, they do not know what to make of it. Literally they're right, for in one of his most important books Tillich wrote unequivocally, "God does not exist."[5]

It would not be fair to a great and sincere Christian to quote this one sentence alone without some effort to elucidate why it was written. The chief reason why Professor Tillich denied the existence of God was not that he was an atheist, as the words seem to say, but that he believed that God is too exalted for the concept of existence to apply. God, whom he worshiped, seemed to Tillich to be above the polar opposites of both essence and existence. He was trying to say, within the limitations and inevitable misunderstandings of human language, that God is *incomparable* to all other realities. He thought it a kind of blasphemy to apply to God the same categories we apply to created things. His meaning is clearer if we expand the controversial brief quotation. "God does not exist. He is being-itself, beyond essence and existence. Therefore, to argue that God exists is to deny him."

Once Tillich had made this statement, it was echoed by hundreds of speakers and writers. For the present purpose one illustration will suffice. William Robert Miller, reviewing Martin Buber's *On Judaism*, says, "There is nothing 'religious' here in a conventional sense, nothing about belief in the existence of a divine being, but rather a prophetic definition of the reality of God."[6]

[5] *Systematic Theology* (Chicago: University of Chicago Press, 1951) , p. 205.
[6] *Saturday Review*, February 10, 1968, p. 34.

In the magnificent character of Paul Tillich the rejection of existence as applied to God exhibited a certain nobility, but this has declined visibly in the intervening years, for the idea of nonexistence becomes even more confusing when it appears at second and third hand. For example, though the words quoted from an article in the *Saturday Review* were written with evident admiration, we have a right to ask seriously whether they have any meaning. Is it intelligent to speak of the "reality of God" if God does not "exist"? Surely what is nonexistent is delusory or imagined; what does not exist has only subjective reference. We speak of Mr. Pickwick, but we are well aware that such a character does not and never did exist, except in the mind of Charles Dickens and his readers. The former's brilliant imagination should never blind us to the fact that there is a difference in kind between what is merely imagined and what really *is*. There is no reason why the same distinction should not apply to discourse about God, for there are many false gods. What a sincere seeker wants to know is whether the Father of Jesus Christ, the One who cares even for the sparrow, really exists or is simply a dream of poor frustrated and lonely men. Freud, as we all know, believed the latter.

No amount of definition of the "reality of God" is worth anything if God is not. The question of divine existence, far from being trivial or merely "religious," as the current cant has it, is intrinsic to the whole problem of the nature of reality, which we shall never solve, but which we can know in part. We are not helped in the least by calling God "Being" rather than "a Being." There is a confused notion to the effect that to call God "a Being" is to limit Him, but this consequence must be boldly faced. Of course God is limited, if by that we mean that He is not everything. He is not sin; He is not nature; He is not finite man. The only possible justification for the rejection of such negatives would be the acceptance of an implicit pantheism; but all pantheism, as

C. S. Lewis has taught us so clearly, is intellectually immature. Though for theism the problem of evil is a difficulty, for pantheism it is a disaster.

Part of the intellectual excitement of the recent past is the emergence of critical studies which succeed in putting the question of God's existence in a new light. Recognizing the ambiguity of the word "is," several thinkers, both Roman Catholic and Protestant, have challenged directly the once popular notion that "existence" is inappropriate in reference to God and have concluded that the plain man is right when he says simply, "God exists." The Roman Catholic thinker who has helped most in this effort is Jacques Maritain,[7] while the leading Protestant thinker in regard to this crucial issue is Helmut Gollwitzer. We have reason to be particularly grateful for Gollwitzer's chapter called "The Necessity of 'is' Propositions." This sensitive thinker appreciates fully the motives of those who have hesitated to use the same language in reference to God as they use in reference to created things, but he goes on to show with remarkable clarity that this is not the final word, for the denial of the existence of God leaves the door open to pantheism. The conclusion is that "in face of this disproportionality between the being of God and the being of the world the wonder of the creation consists precisely in the fact that he, who alone 'is' from eternity to eternity, calls into being that which 'is not.' "[8] Following this Gollwitzer says, "It is a sign of grace that we can predicate the words 'being' and 'existence' both of God and of the creation." He quotes with approval the words of Karl Barth, "It is the existence of God that is the criterion of general existence."

Sometimes the question is asked of a Christian, "Does God

[7] Maritain's book is *Existence and the Existent* (New York: Collier Books, 1962), p. 26.

[8] Helmut Gollwitzer, *The Existence of God as Confessed by Faith* (Philadelphia: Westminster Press, 1965), p. 210.

exist as a stone exists?" and the Christian answer is, "Yes, He does." That is, this is the answer providing we claim that God exists at all, in an objective manner, and is not a mere projection of our wishes. God and the stone have, of course, widely different attributes, but, unless the atheist is right, neither is illusory. The confusion arises because people sometimes find it difficult to make a logical distinction between the fact of existence and the particular qualities of whatever exists. If Christ is trustworthy, as we believe that He is, God does not have the physical characteristics of a stone, and He would not be God if He had, but the point of intelligent belief is that both physical and nonphysical existences are meaningful. The modest Christian believer is now liberated, in view of reflections of contemporary scholars, from the pressure of feeling that it is not respectable to speak of God's existence. Since there is evidence that we are moving back to the main stream of Christian thought, upholders of Basic Christianity need no longer be intimidated.

The second major cause of confusion is what may rightly be called the cult of antisupernaturalism. Readers of Bishop Robinson's phenomenally popular book will remember that he began by trying to debunk the idea of "God out there."[9] Admitting that civilized people do not think of God as being up in the sky, he went on to assert that the very idea of God as being independent of the physical universe must now be likewise abandoned. "But the signs are," he wrote in 1963, "that we are reaching the point at which the whole conception of a God 'out there,' which has served us so well since the collapse of the three-decker universe, is itself becoming more of a hindrance than a help."

It is easy to see how perplexing this was to readers who had learned to respect the Biblical message, "They shall perish, but thou shalt endure," (Ps. 105–26, and Heb. 1:11). If the

---

[9] John Robinson, *Honest to God*, (Philadelphia: Westminster Press, 1963), pp. 15, 16.

Bishop is right, God is limited to the natural order and to whatever is in human experience. He was not saying that he did not believe in God, but that he did not believe in God in a supernatural sense.

The problem is the ancient one of immanence and transcendence. By immanence we mean the indwelling of the divine in the world; by transcendence we mean that the divine reality is not limited to our natural order. Historically, Basic Christianity has stressed both immanence and transcendence,[10] but confusion has come in our time by the virtual denial of transcendence. The person who believes that God is merely "in here" is departing significantly from the witness of Christ, who in His most personal prayer addressed the Father as "Lord of Heaven and Earth," thus including both sides of the divine character.

We always go wrong whenever we affirm one of these without the other. If God is only immanent, He ends when the finite world ends; if God is only transcendent, He cannot be known, and is not active in His created world. Immanence without transcendence involves a denial of full objectivity; transcendence without immanence makes God wholly inscrutable, and not involved in events. Here we can be helped by the clarity of Charles Davis, who, in the broadening of his sympathies, has not lost the sharpness of theological distinctions which was provided by his Roman Catholic education. "The Christian God," he says, "is Creator. That means that he is distinct by transcendence from everything else. Transcendence is not an image of God, but an affirmation about him. What, then, is affirmed? First, that God is not to be identified with the universe or with anything that is part of it."[11]

10 Witness two remarkable chapters in *Nature, Man and God,* by William Temple. Chap. X is called "The Transcendence of the Immanent," while the title of Chap. XI is "The Immanence of the Transcendent."

11 *A Question of Conscience, op. cit.,* p. 22.

Part of the difficulty which modern man faces is that the idea of "God inside" is really attractive to him, as it ought to be. But there is serious danger in this emphasis because it is easy to go on to conclude that the "God inside" is all there is, and this in the end means spiritual disaster. It is a shame that G. K. Chesterton is not much read today, for he understood the danger and expressed it vividly. "Of all horrible religions," he wrote, "the most horrible is the worship of the god within. Anyone who knows anybody knows how it would work; anyone who knows anyone from the Higher Thought Center knows how it does work. That Jones shall worship the god within him turns out ultimately that Jones shall worship Jones."[12] Real religion has to do, of course, with the inner life, but if that is all there is, even the inner life will, itself, wither. "Christianity," Chesterton added, "came into the world firstly in order to assert with violence that a man had not only to look inwards, but to look outwards, to behold with astonishment and enthusiasm a divine company and a divine captain." This is the sort of strong medicine that modern man requires when the confident assaults of the anti-supernaturalists tend to intimidate him.

Now a contemporary voice has been raised, in the mood of Chesterton, to assist in the liberation of Christian minds. David Cairns has written a powerful little book which is a study of divine transcendence, to which he has given the appropriate title *God Up There?*[13] Cairns has shown that it is possible to be both clear and profound in dealing with a difficult and important subject. Like Gollwitzer he gives the Biblical understanding of God the kind of intellectual support which has been all too rare in our generation, for he helps us to see why it is that the Christian faith, in its periods of vitality, has been wholly unabashed in its supernaturalism.

[12] G. K. Chesterton, *Orthodoxy* (New York: John Lane Co., 1909) , p. 138.
[13] Edinburgh: St. Andrews Press, 1967.

It is because the Christian is a man who refuses to worship either nature or himself. Intrinsic to the faith is the conviction that this world, including the human race, is not the whole of reality, and having been created, it is neither autonomous nor independent. The world depends upon God, but God does not depend upon the world.

The third major attack on the specifically Christian conception of God in our generation has been that of impersonalism. Christ, we know, approached the Father in a thoroughly personal fashion, especially in His prayers. But countless contemporary men and women have become convinced that they cannot, with intellectual respectability, follow Christ in this regard. The chief instrument of their attack has been a use of the word "anthropomorphic," which merely means "after the fashion of a man." They are told that if they employ the metaphor "father" and think of God as a Person, they are falling back into childish ways. When we say that God is a Person, someone is likely to ask sarcastically, "Do you really think God is a big man up in the sky?"

This must not be brushed aside as unimportant, for the barrier is, in many minds, a real one. The point to remember is that the only genuine alternative to "personal" is "impersonal" and if God is not a Person, Christ is wrong. Even if there are some people, somewhere, who think of God anthropomorphically, that is not the worst mistake they could make, because to think of God impersonally is infinitely worse. C. S. Lewis brings a characteristic breath of common sense into the discussion by asking, "What soul ever perished for believing that God the Father really has a beard?"[14] Those who take the basic message of the Bible seriously believe that God's thoughts are not our thoughts (Isa. 55:8, 9), and that, though man exists in God's image, God does not exist in ours. The difference is crucial! There may have been

14 *Letters to Malcolm, op. cit.,* p. 22.

a time when anthropomorphism was a clear and present danger, but it certainly is not one now. Furthermore, as Alec Vidler has noted, the very persons who so stress this danger actually fall into it in subtle ways of their own. "To think of God as the Life Force, or as cosmic energy, or as the Absolute or as the Eternal Values or as the Moral Law, is not to rise above anthropomorphism, but to describe God in a human though nonpersonal manner."[15]

The chief confusion, and a confusion which can be dispelled, seems to arise from the fact that many people think of "personal" and "bodily" as identical conceptions, when the opposite is the truth. Part of the difficulty arises when we say "He came in person," by which we sometimes mean "He came physically"; but this usage is already largely obsolete. In our contemporary language, when we speak of a person we mean one who is a center of consciousness, who is able to be *aware,* who is able to have *purposes,* who is able to *know* and to *care.* Now the Christian conviction is that it would be absurd to suppose that the Creator is denied the powers that mark the brightest of His creatures. If God is not a Person, i.e., if He cannot know a man and John Jones can know that man, God is manifestly inferior to Jones. This is an absurdity which the truly thoughtful individual cannot willingly accept. God may be *more* than a Person and probably is, though we do not really know what that means, but unless He is at least as personal as we are, He is not One to whom we can pray. The good news is that, by the testimony of Christ, God is *completely* what we are *partially.*

"How many scholars know (what I discovered by accident)," says C. S. Lewis, "that when uneducated people say impersonal they sometimes mean incorporeal?"[16] Some think that personality is a limitation and, in the words popularized by J. B. Phillips, they want to resist making God

---

[15] *Christian Belief, op. cit.,* p. 18.
[16] *Letters to Malcolm, op. cit.,* p. 7.

"too small." Though this is fully understandable and even admirable in intent, more careful thought would make us, with Phillips, realize that the most serious danger is that of making God small by making Him less than personal. Everything else in the created world is vastly inferior to a person. Persons, even inadequate and inferior persons, are in a deep sense superior to all the stars. "It is not from space that I must seek my dignity," says Pascal, "but from the government of my thought. I shall have no more if I possess worlds. By space the universe encompasses and swallows me up like an atom; by thought I comprehend the world."[17]

Fortunately, the personalistic conclusion is the major conclusion of Christian thinkers. "Unless," says Alec Vidler, "God is both knowable and personal, in the sense that personal communication with Him is possible, we can hardly have any personal interest in His existence."[18] John Coburn, a distinguished American theologian, reaches the same unequivocal conclusion. "God," says Coburn, "is a Person. He is infinitely more than this, but He is at least this . . . if you think of God primarily as a person then when you speak to Him you can say 'you' and 'I'."[19]

In one of his later books, Bishop Robinson makes explicit what many readers had already suspected. In discussing "contemporary prayer style," he speaks of it as a "response to the whole life as 'Thou,'" but complains of its weakness in that it tends to be personalistic, "envisaging God as a separate Thou."[20] This is one of the most revealing passages in all that this popular author has written, for it shows precisely where the issue lies. The passage just quoted demonstrates

17 *Pensées*, No. 348.
18 *Christian Belief, op. cit.*, p. 25.
19 John B. Coburn, *Prayer and Personal Religion* (Philadelphia: Westminster Press, 1957) , p. 12.
20 John Robinson, *But That I Can't Believe* (London: Collins, 1967) , p. 158. In this same book Bishop Robinson totally renounces the idea that God is "a Being" (p. 88) .

one of the chief points of difference between Bishop Robinson and the central heritage of the Christian faith, for in the main stream of Christian thought God has always been envisaged as a "separate Thou." A nonseparate Thou would indeed be a mystery.

To the woman at the well Christ said, "God is a Spirit" (John 4:24, A. V.). The more we analyze the language, the more we realize that this is identical in meaning with what we say today when we affirm, "God is a Person." There has been, through the years, a change in meaning of both person and spirit, with the consequence that person has become the less confusing term today. The word spirit has come to be a kind of abstraction, employed when we refer, for example, to the "spirit of Liberalism." It has, accordingly, lost some of its concreteness, whereas "person" has retained and even accentuated this important element.

There is no way in which we can exaggerate the importance of the word "Thou" as an indication of the depth of religious experience. One excellent definition of a person is: any being to whom the word "thou" may be meaningfully addressed. In some ways the question of the character of God is just as crucial as that of His existence, for God might truly exist and yet not *care*. No one has understood this better or expressed it more brilliantly than did Pascal:

The God of Christians is not a God who is simply the author of mathematical truths, or of the order of the elements; that is the view of heathens and Epicureans. He is not merely a God who exercises His providence over the life and fortunes of men, to bestow on those who worship Him a long and happy life. That was the portion of the Jews. But the God of Abraham, the God of Isaac, the God of Jacob, the God of Christians, is a God of love and comfort, a God who fills the soul and heart of those whom He possesses, a God who makes them conscious of their inward wretchedness, and His infinite mercy, who unites Himself to their inmost soul, who fills it with humility and joy, with confidence and love, who renders them incapable of any other end than Himself.[21]

This eloquent statement is really an elaboration of the insight which came to Pascal on the night of November 23, 1654, when he discovered at first hand that there was something very different from the "God of the philosophers." So revolutionary was this experience that the famous thinker wrote an account of it and sewed it into the lining of his coat.

Perhaps some contemporary inquirers may be assisted in their search by a point made by that able scholar, Donald Baillie, when he wrote, "God is the only perfectly personal being."[22] God is the "Eternal Thou," because he is also the "Eternal I." He is the One who can say "I am," (Exod. 3:14). The Christian who, through Christ, has a glimpse into reality, is convinced that the most real being in the universe is not brute power, and because compassion is more important than is power, all talk of the end of theism is premature. "The Christian," says Gollwitzer, "must not be ashamed of this 'theism,' because the God in whom he believes has not been ashamed to become a 'personal God,' to stoop to encounter him as person to person."[23]

There is reason for hope in the way in which the emphasis upon God as the Living and Personal God unites thinkers who are otherwise as far apart as Gollwitzer and Bultmann. Bultmann's witness is particularly impressive. While it is true, as Bonhoeffer said, that Bultmann exhibits the old liberal tendency of reduction of Jesus' words, there is one

21 *Pensées*, No. 555.
22 *God Was in Christ* (London: Faber & Co.) , p. 43. The famous Professor of St. Andrews was the brother of John Baillie.
23 *Existence of God as Confessed by Faith*, op. cit., p. 43.

point at which he makes no reduction at all, and that is in his understanding of God as a person.

A man [he writes], can know that in this actual life of his he is confronted and claimed by a "Thou." Indeed it is in reality only this claim which gives him his life as a self. And that he . . . knows himself to be claimed by an inescapable "Thou," means that he knows of God, and of God as a Person who speaks to him as "thou."[24]

The testimony of Bultmann and others like him completely turns the edge of the "reproach of anthroporphism." It is not anthropormorphic to address God as "Thou," as Christ did, because anything less is crude reductionism of our concept of the divine character. It is not the affirmers but rather the deniers of divine personality who are limiting God. The ancient word "person," referring to a mask, need not deter us, since it is the contemporary meaning that counts now. We must be on our guard, not merely against seeing God in our own image, but also against turning Him into something *inferior* to our image. That is worse than heresy; it is blasphemy! It is to claim, beyond anything we really know, that God is so ineffable that He is incapable of personal intercourse with finite beings. David Read is speaking as the strongest exponents of the Christian faith have long spoken when he says, "By affirming 'personality' of God the Christian faith is concerned that we talk about the Deity in the highest terms we know."[25]

Though there are people who seem to be puzzled about calling God "Father" as Jesus did, this need not be a problem. It is exactly on a par with the use of the personal pronoun in that, however inadequate such terms may be, any

24 Rudolf Bultmann, *Jesus and the Word* (London: Fontana Books, 1958), p. 147.
25 David H. C. Read, *The Christian Faith,* (New York: Charles Scribner's Sons, 1956), pp. 57-58.

known alternatives are manifestly inferior. The intelligent person who follows Christ's example in calling God "Father" is well aware that he is employing a metaphor and that no metaphor is ever perfect, though such figures are necessary if understanding is to be achieved. God is "He" because He is not "it," and God is "Father" because He is not uncaring. The point of the usage is that a true father cares for the child. Modern Christians are well aware that many human fathers are inadequate in this regard, and that some children have never known a good father, but when we adopt Christ's practice we are not reading back into the divine order our own inadequate standards. What we demonstrate in our human fatherhood is essentially a pale reflection of the divine paternity.

There are many good reaons for knowing that God, far from being a fantasy of our minds, really exists, but no reason is more compelling than that which is involved in understanding what it is to be a person. If we, as modern men and women, begin with experienced fact rather than with speculation, we are wise to stress the known fact that persons actually exist. We know this because *we* are persons. Though we do not know, and may never be able to know, whether there are thinking, self-conscious and partly self-directing beings anywhere else in the sidereal universe, we know that such beings exist in this century on one of the smaller planets, in orbit around one particular sun. This may seem too obvious to mention, because it is common knowledge, but it is certainly not too obvious to examine. It is, indeed, one of the most important of all known facts.

While we are ignorant in countless ways, and may always be so, we are aware that at one point in the total universe there exist beings so radically superior to merely physical existence that they clearly belong to another order of reality. We know that in addition to bodies, such as the forms of rocks, which do not feel, and in addition to animals, which do not make moral distinctions, there are beings who are able to entertain conscious purposes and to care. Though they are not really good, they at least *know* that they are not good. Though they die, they know that they die. I can never cease to wonder at the fact that such beings exist in an apparently unfeeling world and that I am one of them. I do not know very much, but at least I know that ours is a world which includes different levels, and that those beings who are persons illustrate all of the known levels, since they combine bodies, minds, and spirits. It was in reference to these levels that Pascal demonstrated his greatest insight. "The infinite distance between body and mind," he says, "is a symbol of the infinitely greater distance between mind and caring, for caring is supernatural." Both steps are great, though the second is the greater.

All bodies, the firmament, the stars, the earth and its kingdoms, are not equal to the lowest mind; for mind knows all these and itself; and these bodies nothing.

All bodies together, and all minds together, and all their products, are not equal to the least feeling of caring. This is of an order infinitely more exalted.

From all bodies together, we cannot obtain one little thought; this is impossible and of another order. From all bodies and minds, we cannot produce a feeling of the charity; this is impossible, and of another and supernatural order.[26]

Anyone who meditates long and reverently on the amazing emergence of both the second and third orders, which is something no one can deny, is bound to ask, as Pascal did, what kind of world it must take to produce such an emergence. By its fruits the world is known! To reason

26 *Pensées*, No. 792.

forward, which we call prediction, is highly fallible, but reasoning backward from effect to adequate cause is the very stuff of practical reason, without which we could not operate a single day and without which science would be impossible. It does not give certainty, but we do not have certainty anyway, except within a closed mathematical system. Reason from effect to probable cause is a necessity not only for intelligent living, but for any understanding of the world. The method is to start, not with what is deemed desirable, but with what *is,* and to proceed from there to establish the postulates required if what is experienced is to make sense. This is the essence of Kant's method of practical reason and a crucial part of what is called the critical method. Kant asked what postulate is required to make sense of the experience of "I ought." Now we ask what postulate is required to make sense of the experience of every person who can truly say, "I am."

Here is the most difficult problem to be faced by the person who seeks to deny that God really is. He is forced to adopt the credulity of one who believes that caring can emerge from a fundamentally uncaring world. While the Christian is faced by the perplexing problem of evil, the unbeliever is faced by the vastly more difficult and more baffling problem of personality, in what he believes to be an utterly impersonal world. A believer believes in God partly because he is unable to make a leap of faith as great as the atheist is forced to make. The Christian believer is convinced that the quality of love cannot have come except from One who is at the same time both the Fountain of all being and the One who loves.

One of the most important yet most dangerous affirmations of the Bible is: "God is love" (I John 4:8). It is important because it is a striking and memorable way of saying that God is like Christ. It is an effort to make clear, not only that God is loving, but also that His loving concern is so absolutely intrinsic to His nature that it is really part of the definition. Though all this is desirable, it does not eliminate the intellectual danger that comes in the consequent tendency to equate God with love. Some acquaintance with elementary logic ought to enable us to recognize the fact that simple conversion of such a proposition is illicit, but we nevertheless fall into this fallacy. Accordingly, many appear to suppose that we can truly say, "Love is God." The danger of this is particularly great when there is a constant temptation to impersonalize. Some people admit that they like to repeat "God is love" precisely because love is an abstraction rather than a concrete being. They think they have found in this an escape from the anthropomorphism which they so greatly fear.

The conversion of the Biblical proposition is simply erroneous, because not all love is godly by any stretch of the imagination. There is love of the world and, far worse, love of self. Love may easily decline into mere sentimentality and in fact often does so. It may, in many contemporary minds, become a synonym for lust. It is the part of realism to recognize an intrinsic distinction between what men know as love and the Divine Lover.

As we analyze the phenomenon of personality which we ourselves illustrate, we can see that freedom is part of the meaning of this level of existence, for we belong to an order in which goodness is never forced. In short, though God has made us in His image, in that we have the privilege of sharing in creation and thereby making a real difference in the course of events, we are always free to resist Him. Herein lies the reality of sin, which if we did not know it in any other way we could always recognize at first hand in ourselves. God has taken moral freedom so seriously

that He has made men able to oppose His will. The essence
of sin appears when a person settles for love of self more
than for the love of God or love of his neighbor. Though
our freedom is real, it is not unconditional, for the Living
God, who is like Christ, never lets us alone but stands
at each door and knocks endlessly. He speaks even when
we do not listen or when we refuse to hear.

The two contrasting facts of God and human sin were
never far below Pascal's threshold of consciousness.

"The Christian religion [he wrote], teaches men these two truths;
that there is a God whom men can know, and that there is a
corruption in their nature which renders them unworthy of Him.
It is equally important to men to know both these points; and it
is dangerous for man to know God without knowing his own
wretchedness, and to know his own wretchedness, without knowing the Redeemer who can free him from it."[27]

If, with Pascal, we can know and appreciate these two
truths we still have a long way to go, but we are certainly
on the road. We still have many problems to solve, but
we are at least saved from both meaninglessness and pride.
Through making use of the fulcrum some burdens are
already lifted.

27 *Pensées*, No. 555.

CHAPTER IV

THE REALITY OF PRAYER

*After all, man knows mighty little, and may some
day learn enough of his own ignorance to fall down
and pray.*

—HENRY ADAMS

Only in maturity did there dawn upon me the tremendous
significance of the fact that Jesus prayed. This came finally
as something which tipped the balance in my intellectual
struggle. Though I already felt deeply the importance of
prayer, I felt to an equal degree the obstacles involved
in its practice. Especially did I sense the problem of an
apparent conflict between belief in effective prayer and
belief in natural law. But when I realized that Christ
was my center of certitude, and that Christ actually prayed,
all was different. The record shows that He prayed at
each serious crisis of His public career; even the last words
on the cross were words of prayer, "Father, into thy hands
I commit my spirit!" (Luke 24:46) According to one account, He prayed all night before undertaking the decisive
task of choosing the Twelve on whom so much would
depend (Luke 6:12).

If a careful reader goes through the Gospels with pen
in hand, marking every passage referring to prayer, he

is bound to be surprised at the number of his markings. "Nowhere in the religious literature of the world," wrote John Baillie, "can we find stronger statements about the power and efficacy of prayer than we find in the preaching of Jesus."[1] Some religious literature even outside Christianity deals with prayer, but no advocate surpasses Christ in His confidence. In the extreme form of His teaching He said that men "ought always to pray and not lose heart" (Luke 18:1). This conception of continuous and undiscouraged prayer is presented in the form of a parable in the story of the importunate widow. The clear message of the parable is that, when we have prayed and prayed with no apparent result, we are to go on praying harder. When the medicine fails, take more of it! We can easily see that such a practice has about it an apparent absurdity, yet it is one at which Christ is not abashed.

Christ's understanding of the nature of prayer accentuates both its importance and its intellectual difficulties. In both His teaching and His practice, prayer is understood as utterly different from talk *about* God, for prayer is talk *with* God. Such communion is clearly the boldest enterprise in which a human being can engage. To have direct mental intercourse with another finite person is an amazing step, and would seem so to us if we had the wit to see clearly how great the chasm is between one mind and another; but to have intercourse with the Infinite Person is a far greater step. Whenever we actually pray, in the sense which Christ advises, we are seeking to bridge temporarily the chasm between the human and the divine. This does not mean that we, in our essential finitude, become like God, but it does mean that communication with Him is possible. If this is so, and Christ taught that it is, then those who speak of God as the "Absolutely Other" are simply wrong.

1 *Christian Devotion, op. cit.,* p. 43.

Sinful as we undoubtedly are, we are made sufficiently in God's image to have some communion with Him. Jumbled and poor as the reception is, some messages actually come through. When we communicate with our neighbors, learning a little of what is in their thoughts, we leap from one center of consciousness to another by means of physical signs involving sight, sound, and touch. This is wonderful enough, but it is far more wonderful to communicate with the Living God, for then we operate without the use of sensory media. This is the boldest communication of all because it occurs in direct, unmediated fashion. Yet, wonderful as it is, Christ seems never to doubt its reality. When we wonder whether the supposed communication is mere fantasy, we look again at Christ and we are reassured.

The person who has not examined the Gospel record carefully is bound to be amazed at the boldness of Christ's affirmations about prayer. Some of the most staggering are the following: "I tell you, whatever you ask in prayer, believe that you receive it, and you will" (Mark 11:24); "Again I say to you, if two of you agree on earth about anything they ask, it will be done for them by my Father in heaven" (Matt. 18:19); "If you ask anything in my name I will do it" (John 14:14); "And whatever you ask in prayer, you will receive, if you have faith" (Matt. 21:22). Though these statements are invigorating in their boldness, they are also baffling to many seekers because they seem to be at variance with the facts of experience. Certainly a father and mother often pray for the life of a beloved child, and yet though the two agree the child dies. Since Jesus must have known this, we must probe more deeply if we are to ascertain His meaning.

Prayer, as illustrated by Christ's own example, is gloriously varied. It includes adoration, thanksgiving, petition, interces-

sion. Because it has been almost conventional in our day
to suppose that a really high-minded person will not engage
in petition, it is worth noticing that Christ seemed to
have no such scruples at all. What we call the Lord's
Prayer is really ours rather than His, for He did not need
to ask for forgiveness as we do, but it is significant to
note that it is made up almost entirely of petitions. Perhaps
the most vivid of all petitions, and the one which Christ
openly admired, was that of the publican who merely said,
"God be merciful to me a sinner" (Luke 18:13). This
approved prayer not only provides a justification for petition, but also helps us to emphasize the point that, in
prayer, sincerity is more valuable than fancy words. Indeed
prayer, in the Christian sense, is not really a matter of
words at all. Words may of course be employed, but they
are always incidental.

Another mark of Christ's boldness about prayer is the
lack of limitation on what He asked for. This is particularly
surprising to modern people, many of whom have come
to the conclusion that, while it is suitable to pray for
peace of mind or freedom from temptation, it is not suitable
to pray for material things. Christ, we should note, revealed
no such scruples. Far from limiting prayer to concern for
spiritual welfare, He frankly advised His followers to pray
for daily bread, and what is more material than bread?
This observation may bring relief to many troubled minds.
If anything is worth worrying about, it is worth praying
about, and it is certainly dishonest to claim to be more high-
minded than we really are. If a man is troubled by lack of
money needed to support his loved ones, why not share these
troubles with the Father? We are told in one of the epistles
to let our requests be made known unto God "in everything" (Phil. 4:6).

Equally important is the recognition that Christ practiced

intercession for the absent and thereby supported it. Such intercessory prayer was made for those who might not have been conscious of the fact that prayer for them was occurring, the clearest illustration of this being in reference to the leader of the Apostles. "Simon, Simon, behold, Satan demanded to have you, that he might sift you like wheat, but I have prayed for you that your faith may not fail" (Luke 22:31, 32). This example is made all the more difficult by the clear fact that the prayer was not answered affirmatively, at least not for the moment. The sad truth is that Peter's faith *did* fail, that he turned out to be cowardly and denied his Lord. It is likewise shocking to remember that Christ's own prayer for Himself in the Garden of Gethsemane was not answered affirmatively. His prayer was, "Father, if thou art willing, remove this cup from me; nevertheless not my will, but thine, be done" (Luke 22:42). Sadly we must admit that the cup was not removed. Though this does not present an insoluble problem, it does present a difficulty which the honest believer ought not to try to evade. At least it teaches us that a simple answer will not suffice. On another level, we can see that Christ prayed for the unity of His followers in subsequent years (John 17:21), but much of the affirmative answer has thus far been postponed. There has been endurance, amazing endurance in spite of almost incredible odds; the gates of hell have not prevailed; but the unity of Christians, for which Christ prayed, is still elusive. The point to remember, however, is that Christ did not allow differences in either space or time to hinder His intercessory prayer.

There is no doubt that there is serious opposition to prayer in our generation, but it is unhistorical to suppose that this is anything new. In our admiration for the ancient Stoic teachers, we sometimes forget that classic Stoicism was opposed to prayer. Almost any Stoic philosopher would have been profoundly shocked at Christ's parable of the importunate widow. Indeed, the contrast between their system and that of the early Christians is so marked that it is not really surprising that the Athenian Stoics looked upon their Christian visitors with condescension (Acts 17:18). The chief reason why Stoics in any age, including our own, are opposed to prayer is that theirs is a philosophy of acquiescence. Since, according to them, the chief virtue is acceptance, it is wrong to keep asking for things. They believe that the person who asks is merely demonstrating thereby that he is not yet resigned to what God wills.

The Stoic of any generation need not deny the existence of God; what he rejects is the Christian insistence that, in communion with God, prayer can make or should make an objective difference. There is no doubt that many of us, if we examine our positions fearlessly, will find that we are closer to Epictetus than we are to Christ. We tend to place more emphasis, in our prayers, upon acceptance of "that which cannot be changed" than upon the importunity of the widow who sought to change "that which can be changed."

The serious problem which countless persons feel in regard to prayer is that which relates to the will of God. As we hear it in popular dialogue, the objection proceeds somewhat as follows: "Since this is God's world, His will is bound to be done. If He wills war and disease, then war and disease will occur. Because we are poor finite creatures, we cannot change the course of events except perhaps by our own free will, in matters which pertain exclusively to ourselves. How could my little prayer possibly make a difference? Do we really expect that the divine purpose will be altered because of what we happen to think we need? Is it not grossly presumptuous for a mere human being, a mite on a minor planet, to try to instruct the Lord of heaven and earth? Prayer, then, is either ineffective or superfluous! If what we ask is inconsistent with God's will it will not be done; if it is consistent with His will, it will occur anyway, whether we pray or not."

Any Christian who has not engaged in this internal dialogue is hardly alive, for the problem thus raised is genuine and certainly not easily solved; if the honest Christian refuses to face it he is an unfaithful steward of the gospel. Fortunately, we do not have to confront it without assistance, since it has been recognized for many centuries. Some of the clearest answers have been made in the twentieth century, particularly in the writings of Harry Emerson Fosdick, George Buttrick, William Temple, and John Baillie. There are many men and women still living who report, with gratitude, the help received years ago when, as college students, they first encountered Fosdick's remarkable book, *The Meaning of Prayer*. I myself read it while I was an undergraduate, and was so greatly aided that I was subsequently enabled to neglect the ignorant attacks on this particular author which I was later bound to hear. The gratitude which so many felt then for Fosdick's ideas arose primarily from the fact that he enabled them to continue as followers of Christ without any loss of intellectual integrity. And it was in relation to the problem about the will of God that the help was most striking. One significant thing about it is that it is not at all obsolete, being quite as relevant today as when it was written earlier in this century.

We must have an answer to the critic who says, "It is absurd to try to change the will of God, for if we believe in Him at all, we necessarily believe that He is already ordering all things for the best." We are making the beginning of an answer when we point out that the position just enunciated begs the question. Do we know enough about God's will to be sure that it is always done? As soon as we ask that question, we begin to have some light. The fact seems to be that God's will is *not* always done. I have no doubt that He has a will for my life, but I am quite sure that I frustrate it time and again. The possibility of the frustration of God's will is a necessary corollary of the truth that there is a sense in which men and women are really free. Not only are we free to initiate action; we are also free to resist.

It is apparently a serious mistake to think of God's will as something fixed and inflexible, but we make this particular mistake whenever we fall back into mechanistic ways of thinking which fail to rise to the level of the truly personal. The clue to a solution lies in the recognition that we are persons and that God is a Person. Of course it does no good to pray to a machine, but God is not a machine. He is, by contrast, the interested and undismayed Lover, and He is such because He is like Christ. This does not mean, of course, that He requires information. It is fatuous for the person who makes an inaugural prayer to inform God that the date is the twentieth of January. In the same fashion we can be sure that God already understands our hearts, our sins, our motives, our regrets. "There is not a word in my tongue, but, lo, O Lord, thou knowest it altogether" (Ps. 139:4).

If God already knows what we want and, more importantly, knows what we *need*, why tell Him? Because our relationship with the Father is a personal one. Even the poor human parent wants the child to open up his heart without fear or scruples, though most of what is told is already well known. Does not the good husband express his love to his wife, in spite of the fact that she already knows it and has heard the same avowal before? This is not silly; it is merely part of what it means to live on the truly personal level. In prayer, the reverent Christian is not trying to coerce

God; instead he is trying to be open with his Heavenly Father. In Christian experience, prayer is not telling God what to do, for that would be presumptuous; it is, by contrast, telling Him what we think we need. The humble petitioner always adds, at least tacitly, "if it be thy will," because he recognizes his finitude and is sincerely glad that not all of his petitions have been granted. Most of the problems relating to God's will are already solved when we see prayer not as an effort to change it, but as loving communion which may help in the promotion of that will, whereas without the prayer it might be frustrated.

Do we, indeed, really know enough about the order of the universe to be sure that the prayer of a finite person is *not* something that can make a difference? It is not illogical to suppose that it might be part of the divine will for poor, yet free, creatures like ourselves to engage in an experience which is itself a force for change. It is not unreasonable to suppose that the humblest prayer is a necessary link in the chain of objective events. Is it, then, shocking to suppose that the Living God needs us, and even needs our poor prayers? No, as a matter of fact, it is not. Indeed, that seems to be part of the paradox of omnipotence. Whatever God's power may be, we are *needed,* and never more so than when we pray.

A more serious contemporary difficulty about prayer is the idea that effective prayer is incompatible with scientific theory and experience. This is for modern man a harder problem than that of the divine will; though there are millions who cannot believe that the divine will even exists, there are very few who do not respect science. The idea, widespread but seldom really definite and clear, is that we have now outgrown all superstition and consequently reached a stage in which we ask of every event a scientific explanation. Events are already determined because the physical causes already operate. If the present distribution of clouds already determines what tomorrow's weather will be, it is surely a waste of good time to pray for a change of weather. According to this understanding of reality, the saving of so many lives in the evacuation of Dunkirk was not the result of prayers, but a mere coincidence. In the same fashion, if your child contracts polio it is irrational to pray, since the outcome depends upon the skill of the physician and upon nothing else. Prayer, according to this conclusion, may make the one who prays feel better, but it has and can have no objective effect. That this is a position widely taken in the modern world is attested by the fact that numerous readers immediately recognize it as their own.

Because the supposed incompatibility of effective prayer with science is so widely and uncritically accepted, it calls for examination. The first step in careful analysis is a better understanding of science. It is an error to think of science as a set of dogmas, when as a matter of fact it is primarily a method. It is a way of looking at the evidence, of creating hypotheses, and of seeking verification of these hypotheses. In its noblest periods science has been intrinsically open-ended, always willing to reach new conclusions in the light of new evidence. True scientific method can be applied to any subject under inquiry, whether it be the existence of atoms, the age of the Dead Sea Scrolls, or the reported experience of men with the Living God.

The truth is that the supposed intellectual barriers to the acceptance of prayer come, not from science, but from a dogmatic philosophy which is sometimes associated with scientific effort, and is found more among those who superstitiously idolize science than among practicing scientists. This dogmatic philosophy is termed, in our day, "scientism." Whereas the true scientist is open to all evidence, from whatever quarter, the victim of scientism has his mind made up in advance. Even before careful examination, he claims to know already what is impossible. Such a position, when rigorously examined, as it has often been, turns out to be harder to sustain than is usually imagined.

One of the best gifts with which Basic Christianity can provide modern man is intellectual liberation from bondage to dogmatism. Whatever the truth about our world, it is undoubtedly far more wonderful than anything we have thus far understood or even suspected. Our knowledge is, as Santayana said, merely "a torch of smoky pine," which "lights the pathway but one step ahead." If our knowledge is truly fragmentary, it is evidently a mistake to accept intellectual bondage to a closed system, since the world may contain far more than is now envisaged in our little philosophy. Essential to real openness is recognition of the possibility that prayer may be a genuine causal factor, along with other causes, in the course of events in daily life.

"We are all 'conditioned,'" says J. B. Phillips, "by the modern outlook which regards the whole of life as a closed system."[2] In this the wise New Testament scholar has put his finger upon the major source of confusion. The popular view is that events are controlled, not by the purpose of Almighty God, but by a system of wholly impersonal natural laws. The conviction is that these laws are independent and autonomous and consequently cannot be controlled by anything outside themselves. Physical causes, therefore, are seen as the only real ones. If the polio germ exists, it cannot be stopped except by other physical entities. Material causes are thus seen as both necessary and sufficient.

In all frankness, we ought to face the fact that such a naturalistic dogmatism is nothing but disguised atheism, for belief in a God who cannot affect events in the world is really worse than no belief at all. It is easy to delude our-

2 *Your God Is Too Small, op. cit.,* p. 118.

selves by thinking that we believe in God when we do not, and a world view which denies the reality of effective prayer is actually incompatible with belief in God in any meaningful sense. If we are required to choose between this and acknowledged atheism, atheism is far preferable, because it is more honest.

When we begin to look at the world with any genuine humility we realize that it is at least thinkable that there may be invasions into our causal system, for there is nothing illogical about the idea that God is superior to what we call natural law. We are helped along this liberating road when we realize that natural laws do not tell us what *must be,* but are mere generalizations of what, in a very short period of history, has been generally observed to occur. The Christian understands natural law as merely the way in which God's purposive action in our little corner of the universe normally takes place. When I first began to entertain the idea that there is nothing sacred about a closed system, this constituted for me a great emancipation. Before that, I had serious trouble in seeing how prayer could be a genuine force in the chain of events; after that, the major barrier was removed. I was much helped by G. K. Chesterton, partly because his belief in miracles was so utterly unapologetic. "The believers in miracles," he wrote, "accept them (rightly or wrongly) because they have evidence for them. The disbelievers in miracles deny them (rightly or wrongly) because they have a doctrine against them."[3]

This is a good illustration of how critical thought assists the person who has been attracted to Christ and desires, accordingly, to be His follower, but is held back by other considerations. It is conceivable, of course, that Christ's explicit belief in prayer and consequent practice of it were made possible only because He did not have the advantage of

[3] *Orthodoxy, op. cit.,* pp. 278, 279.

living, as we do, in a scientific age. Perhaps His faith, though
wonderfully appealing, is actually obsolete because He did
not know the things which we now know. After all, He
never saw a laboratory or even an observatory. I know of
no way in which a modern man can be liberated from this
unlovely condescension other than by a more thorough examination of the philosophy of science. This is an example
of what is meant by saying that, though reason may not be
sufficient to bring a man to God, it may be effective in re-
moving some of the barriers that keep him away from God.
While this function of reason is primarily negative, it is not,
on that account, insignificant.

Prayer is an activity which can bear full intellectual examination on one important condition, which is that God
is not imprisoned in His own creation. If God *is* imprisoned
in a world which He has made, the things that matter most
are then at the mercy of the things that matter least, and
prayer must be abandoned. If, on the other hand, God is not
imprisoned, if He is marked more by intelligence than by
mechanism, nothing is fixed or inflexible. Above all, if God
is a Person, and if His image, seen in Christ, is an accurate
reflection of His nature, then there is no reason at all to
assert that He cannot act with evident purpose in an unusual
fashion. Once we are liberated from intellectual bondage,
our golden text becomes the words of Christ when He de-
clared, "With God all things are possible" (Matt. 19:26).

Though they are usually handled separately, prayer and
miracle are both better understood if they are handled together. By a miracle a Christian does not mean something
mysterious and unaccountable, but rather an event in which
the redemptive purpose of God is clearly manifest. A miracle
is an alteration in the ordinary course of events which, far
from being puzzling, is a clear evidence of divine purpose in
God's world. If Christ rose from the dead, as the evidence

indicates, that is a miracle. It is a miracle because, in this instance, God chose to intervene directly in the course of events and did so for a transcendently important purpose. If this was necessary to change men's hearts it is not really puzzling, but highly *intelligible*. It means that, because this is God's world and not some impersonal or merely mechanical order, the level of "caring" can impinge upon the level of "bodies." It means, moreover, that ours is a world in which both natural and supernatural causes can operate, and can operate together. If God is, as Christ affirmed, then it is wholly reasonable that He should design events which constitute special revelations of His personal activity, in the long fulfillment of His purpose. A miracle is not a mystery but a revelation. Miracles do not contravene the laws of nature, but reveal the Lawgiver.

No Christian who understands his position settles for the sentimentality of saying that he believes in miracles because *everything* is a miracle. It sounds pious, but merely evades the issue, for it fails to face the sharp difference between classes of events. Of course each natural event, such as the birth of a baby, has about it an element of intrinsic wonder, but that is not the point at issue. Unless Christ was mistaken about Himself, the birth of *one* baby was of a totally different order, because it represented a genuine invasion of the natural order.

The point of this discussion is that prayer and miracle go reasonably together, because every prayer of petition is really a request for a miracle. When I pray for the recovery of my sick child, I am asking God to bring to bear upon the concrete situation something more than what is provided by antibiotics, however valuable these may be and however grateful we may be for their invention. Prayer is, in its very essence, supernatural. The communication with other finite spirits appears to be limited to the employment of sensory organs, but this is not true when the finite person is in real communication with the Infinite Person, for there is no sight, no sound, no tactile sensation. There is, moreover, no absolute limitation at all, such as the speed of light. Indeed, we are in a supernatural area of experience in which the limitations of space and time have no significance whatever. If such an area of experience is denied, the only possible conclusion is that prayer is meaningless; but if the supernatural is denied, Christ is denied, and then He is no longer our fulcrum.

One possible alternative to a frankly supernatural view is that prayer is merely internal discourse. Perhaps, say some, when we engage in prayer we are like the Prodigal Son who "came to himself." This, of course, is a possible hypothesis, but because it would reduce prayer to autosuggestion it is not really worth considering. We should be far more honest if we were to have the courage to renounce prayer completely and say frankly that Christ was deluded. The only conception of prayer that is intellectually valid is that which draws on resources that are not our own.

A more practical problem, some people feel, is that prayer seems like an alternative to work. Prayer, they say, diverts men from the real task at hand and is accordingly harmful. Don't pray about the disease; get a doctor! This looks like common sense, but is it? Why should prayer and work be looked upon as conflicting human enterprises? The truth is that we can pray *while* we work, and we can work while we pray. There is no need whatever to choose between calling a doctor and praying, since it is obvious that any man can do both. It is good to note that, in Christ's teaching about prayer, the alternative to prayer is not work but something very different. The parable of the importunate widow seems to have been told in order to teach men that they "ought always to pray and not to lose heart" (Luke 18:1) . In the

Authorized Version the alternative is translated "to faint." Here, of course, is our trouble. We *do* lose heart; we *are* bored; our lives often seem meaningless. More genuine praying, more real encounter with the Father of our spirits, more willingness to live in an open universe, more genuine listening, far from decreasing the effectiveness of our labor would actually enable us to get more work done. The testimony of thousands of sincere people is that, with prayer, they are able to perform their mundane tasks with less weariness and anxiety. In any case, in the example of Christ, prayer did not lessen but rather enhanced His work of healing broken men and women, both in body and spirit. With Him we can truly say of the worst maladies that afflict mankind, "This kind cannot be driven out by anything but prayer" (Mark 9:29).

When we move from speculation to empirical evidence we cannot avoid the fact that the reports of effective prayer are impressive. There is a deep realism in concentrating our attention, not upon what is possible or impossible, but on what *occurs*. It is hard to neglect the witness of the man who admits that he does not know who it was who healed him, but says simply, "One thing I know, that though I was blind, now I see" (John 9:25). In the face of the abundant evidence of the effectiveness of prayer it is hard to dogmatize. About all the skeptic can do is to reply that, though the result prayed for does sometimes occur, this is a mere coincidence. The solemnity of this confident answer was in one instance somewhat shaken by the humor of William Temple, when he admitted that it was conceivable that the events which occurred in his wonderful and productive life were merely coincidental, but added that the coincidences came more frequently when he prayed!

It must be understood that no thoughtful Christian, and certainly not William Temple, ever supposes that prayer works in a mechanical sense. People die even when there are prayers for their recovery, both on their own part and on the part of those who love them. Though the men of Dunkirk escaped in great numbers, there are others, for whom there are equally fervent prayers, who do not escape. Some who are prayed for come out of the flooded mine shaft; others fail to come out. The kind of evidence involved in effective prayer is not absolute, but it is nevertheless so great, on the part of so many, that anyone concerned with fact and not mere theory cannot neglect it. Therefore the pragmatic advice is: "Be careful what you pray for; it may come to pass!"

When we consider the magnitude of the undertaking in which a finite person proposes to enter into conversation with God Almighty, we are almost overwhelmed. How can it be done, and how shall we begin? Fortunately, the task seems less baffling and the undertaking less presumptuous when we realize that the Father is actually seeking us. One of the greatest contributions of the late Rufus Jones was his coining of the brilliant phrase, "double search." Professor Jones understood that real religion is not merely man's search for God, and not even God's search for man, but always the combination. If God is really seeking people, in order to share His life with those He loves, even when they are unlovable; if there is really One who stands at the door and knocks (Rev. 3:20) ; then man's position is not as hopeless and desperate as it appears. In any case we do not have to initiate the divine-human encounter; our major responsibility is the simpler one of response.

One important lesson to be learned, in trying to engage in prayer which is something more than mere meditation or internal soliloquy, is to recognize that we do not have to wait to begin until all our intellectual problems are resolved. A little thought will show that we start on many lesser enterprises even while some problems are still unsolved. The person who postpones marriage until he is absolutely sure on every point will remain unmarried all his life, and the same applies in choosing a vocation or in any other important decision. After we have used our reason and have honestly faced as many questions as we can envisage, there must in any decision be a final venture of trust as the crucial step is taken. Perhaps this is much of what is meant by Christ's saying that the person who "does not receive the kingdom of God like a child shall not enter it" (Mark 10:15).

We do not know, and we are not likely to know, how it is possible for there to be direct communication between the Divine Mind and the human mind. Like the healed man, we can see even though we do not know the method of seeing. If we have a tolerable way of handling the problem of God's will, and if we see that the idea of a closed universe is not nearly as impressive, when examined, as it at first appears to be, we are ready to start. We are ready to see that it is not irrational to suppose that God's cosmic purpose includes such a self-limitation of His power that some events do not occur apart from the prayers of finite men. Then, with the major barriers lowered, or at least made less formidable, we are ready to learn to pray by praying.

If we take seriously the wisdom about entering as a little child, our prayers need not be grand or polished. It is helpful to know that we shall not be heard for our much speaking (Matt. 6:7). Indeed, a great part of prayer need not involve words at all, for words are not the music, but only the movements of the conductor's baton. As our contemporary world becomes ever more noisy, silence is hard to find, but it can be found if we really prize it. One paradox is that people who complain of noise often actually resist silence, for even when it is blessedly possible it is sometimes rejected. We go into an empty house, where the silence could be healing, but we deny this to ourselves voluntarily by immediately using the telephone or turning on the radio or television. Perhaps we are really afraid of the encounter that silence makes possible! In public worship a brief period of silence sometimes makes people so impatient that they almost leave, for they have forgotten the ancient wisdom, "Be still and know" (Ps. 46:10). In any case it is a poor conversation in which we talk all the time and never listen. Many are grateful to that veteran missionary, E. Stanley Jones, for his frequent reference to his own daily practice of simply asking, "Lord, what do you have to say to me?" and then waiting silently until he hears. Here is a practice in which any person can engage, even though he continues to have intellectual problems which he cannot fully solve. There is no conceivable dishonesty in the effort to listen; it is the acme of humility.

The man who is willing to pray, but realizes that he does not know how to do it, can hardly do better than to start with thanks. The most personal of all of Christ's recorded prayers begins, "I thank thee" (Matt. 11:25). Any person has made a great start on the boldest of enterprises if he sincerely utters three ejaculations: "Thank you!" "Help me!" "Help John and Mary!" Elementary as these may be, they can never become outmoded. Each person, if he is honest, is well aware of blessings far beyond anything he deserves. Any honest person, no matter how strong, recognizes his need and sees that, in fact, he needs all the help he can get.

But the more mature we become the more we concentrate, in our prayers, upon the needs of others. A good many people who have prayed for a long time make it a practice to keep a list of names of individuals for whom they pray, sometimes every day. The prayer groups now organized in prisons encourage each prisoner to keep, in his cell, a list of the others in his group and to pray for each by name at the beginning of each day. After a while the prayer for oneself is only a tiny fraction of total prayer, while prayer for others becomes the major experience. Though we are perfectly right in praying for ourselves, and though we are foolish to claim that we are more high-minded than we actually are, the greater part of prayer ought not to be centered upon our own needs at all. One way to make prayer more real is to begin by contemplating the lives of others and thinking of the help they need. It is then perfectly natural to pray specifically for each individual and not merely for mankind in general.

Ought we to pray alone or with others? Here both the teaching and practice of Christ provide a clear answer. There are times, and perhaps a majority of times, when we ought to pray alone. Christ's practice in this regard is well represented in the New Testament. In the Garden of Gethsemane He prayed alone, even though the apostles were not far distant (Luke 22:41). We know that He went apart to pray in the early morning hours (Mark 1:35). Further, in the Sermon on the Mount, as a clear alternative to the kind of prayer which may be public because it is really ostentatious, He said, "When you pray, go into your room and shut the door and pray to your Father who is in secret" (Matt. 6:6).

Some people have been so impressed by Christ's advice about solitary prayer that they have drawn the wrong conclusion that prayer ought never to be experienced in company with others. But Christ supported both solitary and group experience and exemplified both; they are not, of course, mutually exclusive. The experience on the Mountain of Transfiguration was clearly that of a prayer group (Mark 9:2). Moreover, the moving statement about the presence in the midst is itself an affirmation of the value and necessity of prayer with others. We reach a deep place, indeed, when we hear Christ say, "For where two or three are gathered in my name, there I am in the midst of them" (Matt. 18:20). The most unequivocal promise is made, not concerning the prayer of one, but the prayer of two (Matt. 18:19). The conclusion we must reach is that there is a time to pray alone, and likewise a time to pray with others. What is odd is the idea that it is necessary to choose.

A similar practical question concerns the time of prayer in our program. Should there be particular times devoted to prayer or should we seek to make prayer a continuous experience in all of our conscious moments? Again the clear answer is that we must see the value of both approaches and follow both as best we can. The ideal of continuous prayer is a noble one, but not many are able to claim that they actually practice it. Ideally we should keep prayer always just below the threshold of consciousness, so that it becomes as natural as breathing. Some, like Brother Lawrence in the seventeenth century, seem to have been able to achieve this, but most of us have to admit that we do not. The path of wisdom is to go on trying, without claiming more than the truth. It would be grand if every time a Christian walked into a room or met a new person he should consciously breathe a prayer for help and wisdom. Then we would refuse to recognize any distinction between the sacred and the secular, because work and prayer would be simultaneous. Much of the appeal of Thomas Kelly came because he advocated and practiced prayer of this unbroken kind.[4]

We have made a real advance when we see that continuous prayer is not at all incompatible with prayer at special times. We need the particular occasions for the simple reason that we are not angels. As Dr. Johnson taught, we are so feeble that we need reminders. Unless we fall into the angelic fallacy, we realize that we are sufficiently weak and forgetful to require the establishment of habits of devotion. Kneeling is good, because it may be helpful to pray with the body as well as the mind. Though prayers may come at any time of the day, they appear to help most at bedtime or in the early morning. The great value of prayer at the beginning of each

[4] See *A Testament of Devotion* (New York: Harper & Row, 1946), p. 122.

day is that it provides a marvelous setting for the day's activi-
ties and a preparation for the good and evil that will come.
Especially helpful is the discipline of the "plotted day"
associated with the Iona Fellowship in Scotland. This means
going through the day in prospect, in so far as the individual
is able, and asking guidance at each particular point. This
does not, we may be sure, make the plan of the day inflexible,
but does bring the details into order, because the big things
become big and the small things are seen in their appropriate
insignificance, while almost always new tasks are thereby
discovered.

The best prayer is seldom a hit-and-miss matter, but grows
by the glad acceptance of discipline, which, far from being its
antithesis, is the price of real freedom. Herein lies the deep
wisdom of the Yoke passage (Matt. 11:29, 30). Just as all
empty freedom inevitably turns into bondage, so the acceptance of Christ's yoke sets men free. It does not eliminate
burdens, but because the yoke fits, the burdens actually seem
light. In Christ's teaching the practice of devotion is the first
step of a series in which freedom is the final consequence. "If
you continue in my word, you are truly my disciples, and you
will know the truth, and the truth will make you free" (John
8:31, 32).

Should prayers be written or spontaneous? Again the answer is both. There is great merit in the study of prayers
others have written, and there is equal merit in trying to
write one's own. Almost anyone is helped by writing a few
prayers each year, partly because the very act of writing can
be an exercise in honesty. It is highly important not to lie
when we pray and not to ask for anything, purity for example, which we do not sincerely desire. Writing helps to
avoid wordiness and the repetition of clichés. But to limit
ourselves to written prayers, even the noblest, is a serious
mistake, for we need to break through all forms.

However sure we may be that the best praying is both
spontaneous and original, our very spontaneity and origi-
nality may be enhanced if we deliberately soak ourselves in
the classical models of devotion. Almost anyone will learn to
pray better by immersing himself in *The Imitation of Christ*
or in the collects of the *Book of Common Prayer*. When we
look for the great models we soon recognize the eminence of
the prayers of that superlatively honest man, Dr. Samuel
Johnson. Fortunately, we have many of them in his own
handwriting, preserved in the library of his old college,
Pembroke, at Oxford. Because there are times when each one
of us stands in need of healing, we can hardly fail to feel the
relevance of the following prayer, dated November 5, 1769.

Almighty God, merciful Father, whose providence is over all thy
works, look down with pity upon the diseases of my body, and the
perturbations of my mind. Give thy blessing, O Lord, to the
means which I shall use for my relief, and restore ease to my body
and quiet to my thoughts. Let not my remaining life be made useless by infirmities, neither let health, if thou shalt grant it, be employed by me in disobedience to thy laws; but give me a sense of
my pains, as may humble me before thee; and such remembrance
of thy mercy as may produce honest industry, and holy confidence.
And, O Lord, whether thou ordainest my days to be past in ease
or anguish, take not from me thy Holy Spirit; but grant that I
may attain everlasting life, for the sake of Jesus Christ our Lord.
Amen.[5]

It may be truly said of Dr. Johnson, as he said of Milton,
that "he was born for whatever is arduous."[6] Johnson was
exceedingly tough-minded; he could never believe easily or

[5] The first volume of the ambitious new Yale publication of Johnson's works
includes, in a new arrangement, both his prayers and his extant diaries. For
the prayer printed above see Samuel Johnson, *Diaries, Prayers and Annals*,
(New Haven; Yale University Press, 1958) , p. 124.
[6] Samuel Johnson, *Lives of the Poets: Cowley to Prior* (Garden City, N.Y.
Doubleday Dolphin Books) , p. 144.

lightly; but he saw clearly that if God is, man's noblest undertaking is that of prayer. Much as we prize his other productions, we may prize his prayers longest, for they are essentially dateless. If we seriously wonder whether it is possible, in this life, to be both tough-minded and tender-minded, here is part of our evidence. Integrity and reverent humility are not exclusive options; they go best together.

CHAPTER V

AND THE LIFE EVERLASTING

—————◆—————

Praised be my Lord for our sister, the death of the
body.

—ST. FRANCIS

Man is an animal, but he is more than an animal. If he were
only an animal there is no reason to suppose that he would
ever have discovered that fact. One of the most striking ways
in which a human being is unique among creatures is that,
while all creatures die, man alone knows that he dies. Every
reader of these words is keenly conscious of the prospect of
the cessation of his earthly existence, recognizing that before
many years have elapsed the places of those of us who are
alive today will have been taken by others. We do not know,
beyond a shadow of doubt, whether there will be any human
beings alive a century from now, but we share the certitude
that if there are any earthly inhabitants we shall not be
among them.

The willingness to face the prospect of death is one mark
of man's rationality. No gain will come by either denying or
seeking to evade our intrinsic mortality. We can go even
farther and actually rejoice in the apparent inevitability of
human death, because without it the crowded condition of
our living space would become intolerable. Plato established

106

the pattern of philosophical thinking on this subject when he put into the mouth of his beloved Socrates some words about death which are the exact opposite of morbid or despairing. "And now, O my judges, I desire to prove to you that the real philosopher has reason to be of good cheer when he is about to die, and that after death he may hope to obtain the greatest good in the other world."[1] These words are attributed to Socrates a short time before his execution. The philosopher knew that his gaiety in the face of death was hard for others to understand, but he said that this was because they did not perceive that true philosophers "are always occupied in the practice of dying." By this he meant the process by which we become progressively liberated from the compulsions of the flesh and worldly ambitions. The "practice of dying," in Plato's sense, is what might better be called "Operation Liberation."

Socrates, living more than four hundred years before the Christian era, was called by Justin Martyr a "Christian before Christ." Part of the reason for this was his clear conviction that human death is not a calamity, and that this is because it may reasonably be followed by a conscious existence far more glorious than we now know. The Athenian thinker was so far ahead of his time that he envisaged the life to come as one marked by personal consciousness, including the ability to share both ideas and affection.

What would not a man give if he might converse with Orpheus and Musaeus and Hesiod and Homer? Nay, if this be true, let me die again and again. I myself, too, shall have a wonderful interest in there meeting and conversing with Palamedes, and Ajax the son of Telamon, and any other ancient hero who has suffered death through an unjust judgment; and there will be no small pleasure, as I think, in comparing my own sufferings with theirs. Above all, I shall then be able to continue my search into true and

1 *Phaedo*, 64A.

false knowledge; as in this world, so also in the next; and I shall
find out who is wise, and who is not. What would not a man give,
O Judges, to be able to examine the leader of the great Trojan
expedition; or Odysseus or Sisyphus, or numberless others, men
and women too! What infinite delight would there be in conversing with them and asking them questions![2]

The modern reader, when he appreciates the profundity of
the Socratic conception, naturally adds names meaningful to
himself. Some of us, for instance, may prize the opportunity
to inquire of the Apostle Paul concerning the exact nature of
his "thorn in the flesh," and whether he was ever a married
man. Or we may ask William Shakespeare how a man grow-
ing up in Stratford, with so little formal education, was
nevertheless able to know and do so much. The game that
Charles Lamb and his friends played, according to William
Hazlitt, of naming persons one would like to have seen or
known,[3] is according to Socrates one which, by the grace of
God, will someday be played in reality.

When we grasp Socrates' central conviction, it is easy to see
why Edith Hamilton included a chapter on him in her life of
Christ, *Witness to the Truth*. Even when he knew that he
had only a few more days to live on earth, he reaffirmed his
central faith. "Wherefore, O Judges," he said at the end of
his famous trial, "be of good cheer about death, and know of
a certainty, that no evil can happen to a good man, either in
life or after death." In these words the Athenian was the
clear precursor of the Apostle Paul, who wrote even more
eloquently, "For I am sure that neither death, nor life, nor
angels, nor principalities, nor things present, nor things to
come, nor powers, nor height, nor depth, nor anything else in
all creation, will be able to separate us from the love of God
in Christ Jesus our Lord" (Rom. 8:38, 39).

2 *Apology*, 41A.
3 William Hazlitt, *Winterslow*, Essay II.

When the apostle, in listing the possible barriers to fullness of life, placed death first, he was simply being reasonable. If the decay of the flesh, which is inevitable, is also *final,* human life is a fundamentally tragic episode. There are some good experiences in the earthly life of men and women, but there are also some very bad ones, and no human promise is ever really fulfilled in this life. It is not necessary to go along with the philosopher Thomas Hobbes in saying that human life is "poore, nasty, brutish and short," but Hobbes was only exaggerating what every thoughtful person knows. Some, like Plato, do succeed in living long and fruitful lives, but millions of others are cut off before they see the rewards of their dreams. Some die by torture! If this life is all, only a sentimentalist could call it truly good. A man like Samuel Shoemaker could say, "It's been a great run," but there are countless others who cannot honestly say the same. Instead, they are forced to say with Dr. Johnson that this life is one in which "much is to be endured, and little to be enjoyed." In any case, man is a very cruel animal who, in his lust for power, does terrible things to other men. The chief reason for stressing love is the pragmatic one that so much of our life is obviously unloving.

In the light of such realism, we can understand to some degree the crucial character of the question whether consciousness survives death. If I could know that it does not, if I were certain that Socrates was deluded, I believe I should still try to live out my few days with as much affection and justice as possible, but I doubt if I should be gay. If I could know that there is no further chance for those who meet manifest injustice here, I should understand that I live in a highly irrational world, and in all honesty I must report that my trust in God would be weakened. But I do *not* know this, and furthermore, I have ample reason to conclude that it is not true. On a subject of such transcendent importance for human meaning and happiness, it is the duty of each man to share whatever light he may have.

It is conceivable that the death of the body is final. In that case individual persons may be remembered for a while, but on the whole the reminders grow fainter with the passing of time. This can be verified by the simple act of visiting any old cemetery. The notion that conscious life after death is unnecessary because of what is termed "cultural immortality" is a pathetically confused notion, providing no permanent solution of the human problem. In any case the immortality of memory and influence will come to an end with the running down of our solar system, which according to the Second Law of Thermodynamics is bound finally to occur. In short, cultural immortality, however comforting it may be for a little while, is not really immortality and has nothing in common with the magnificent Christian belief in everlasting life, which holds the climactic position in the Apostles' Creed.

There are few contrasts between the Old Testament and the New which are sharper than that concerning life after death. In the Hebrew faith before the time of Christ, the conception of life after death was fragmentary and shadowy at best, but, with the coming of Christ, all was radically altered. The entire New Testament glows with the conviction that this life is not all and that our best personal experience, far from being ended by the death of the body, can be thereby brought to completion and fulfillment. The new faith is not expressed in isolated passages, but is found in both the Gospels and the Epistles. The most striking feature of Christ's own teaching on this subject is its unqualified and unequivocal confidence. The essence of His position is that, because God really is, and because the whole world, both present and future, is under His fatherly care, we shall be objects of His affection just as much after the death of the body as we were before. Because we could not be objects of His affectionate care if we were not alive, then those who love Him will continue to live. The heart will stop beating, but that it is only a minor incident.

The manner of Christ's approach to these great issues impressed Pascal almost as much as did the substance of His teaching. "Jesus Christ said great things so simply, that it seems as though He had not thought them great; and yet so clearly that we easily see what He thought of them. The clearness, joined with this simplicity, is wonderful."[4] The finest example of this combination is found in the dialogue with the Sadducees, who did not believe in the resurrection. It is in the record of this encounter that we come across the exciting phrase, "sons of the resurrection." The crucial passage, which we owe to Luke's vigilance and perceptiveness, is as follows: "The sons of this age marry and are given in marriage; but those who are accounted worthy to attain to that age and to the resurrection from the dead neither marry nor are given in marriage, for they cannot die any more, because they are equal to angels and are sons of God, being sons of the resurrection. But that the dead are raised, even Moses showed, in the passage about the bush, where he calls the Lord the God of Abraham and the God of Isaac and the God of Jacob. Now he is not God of the dead, but of the living; for all live to him" (Luke 20:34–38) .

For Christ, and for all Christians, belief in continued life following death is clearly a corollary of belief in God. The final belief in the Apostles' Creed comes last, because it is a consequence. If God is not, then there is no reason to believe in the continued existence of finite persons and the subject is not really worth discussing. If God is not, spiritual experience on our planet is a totally unexplained aberration, with no assignable cause, and there is no reason to expect its

4 *Pensées,* No. 796.

continuation after the body has died. If God is not, Lord
Bertrand Russell is right when he says that all the monu-
ments of men's genius will be "buried beneath the débris of a
universe in ruins." But if God really is, as Christ both
believed and revealed, then there is nothing strange at all
about the continued existence of those who are the special
objects of the Father's care. The oddity would be cessation of
existence, since that would mean that God either will not or
cannot keep alive the individuals whose life He prizes.

It must be understood that the life everlasting, as affirmed
by Christians, and as expressed in the entire New Testament,
is unequivocally personal and individual. There is nothing
said about the individual spirit returning to God and being
lost as a drop of water loses its identity when it returns to the
ocean. It is not the mass of humanity, or some abstract
deposit of spirit, that is supremely valued, but rather the
individual person, for it is in the principle of individuality
that value resides. Not sparrows in general, but the individual sparrow is the object of the Father's care. "Not one of
them is forgotten before God" (Luke 12:6). Though spirit
in general is a mere abstraction, individual spirit is concrete,
and God, as represented by Christ, values the concrete. We
do not and probably cannot know the details of the life to
come, but we are assured that it will be a conscious existence,
marked by a true liberation from many of the limitations we
suffer in our brief period of preparation on this earth.

The conviction of the earliest Christians was that they
were, indeed, the children of the resurrection, and this seems
to have provided the most powerful motivation in their total
lives. Since they were engaged, they thought, not merely in a
temporary earthly struggle, but in an eternal undertaking,
every event was thereby potentially glorified. In writing of
this conviction the Apostle Paul, who did not claim to be a
good speaker, but was undoubtedly a most gifted writer, rose

to heights of eloquence. Of the Living Christ he said that his own central purpose was "that I may know him and the power of his resurrection, and may share his sufferings, becoming like him in his death, that if possible I may attain the resurrection from the dead" (Phil. 3:10, 11). It was because this faith was more than mere speculation that it was so evidently marked by power.

The entire mood of the early Christians, in reference to survival beyond the grave, was marked by a combination of confidence and severest agnosticism. They did not allow their confidence, which was complete, to drive them into a position in which they claimed to know more than had been given them. Perhaps the most beautiful expression of this combined mood is one sentence in John's First Letter: "Beloved, we are God's children now; it does not yet appear what we shall be, but we know that when he appears we shall be like him, for we shall see him as he is" (I John 3:2). John Greenleaf Whittier was writing in conscious association with this humble mood when, disclaiming any detailed knowledge, he reported that he was "Assured alone that life and death, His mercy underlies." In the new life that is waiting for the sons of the resurrection there will be nothing to disappoint, though there may be much to surprise.

Because Christian faith is so often caricatured, Christians being supposed to expect gold-paved streets in heaven, it is necessary to clarify this point. No mature Christian ever thinks that he knows what heaven is like, and most reverent people recognize how unprofitable all speculation on this point really is. On this, as on so many subjects, John Baillie spoke and wrote with a sure touch, avoiding the errors of both overconfidence and irreverence. "No doubt," he said, "it will all be utterly different from anything we have ever imagined or thought about it. No doubt God Himself will be unimaginably different from all our present conceptions of

Him. But he will be unimaginably different only because He will be unimaginably better. The only thing we do certainly know is that our highest hopes will be more than fulfilled, and our deepest longings more than gratified."[5]

Though it is widely supposed that the Christian belief in life everlasting is a mere hope with no intellectual justification, this is erroneous. The teaching of the New Testament on this important subject is clear, but it does not stand alone. The rationality of the belief depends, not upon absolute proof, which we have learned not to expect anywhere, but rather upon a balance of alternatives. The reasonableness of continued life exceeds the reasonableness of the finality of physical death. The popular idea that the believer is merely tender-minded, while the denier is tough-minded, is one of the current notions which will not bear careful examination. Faith in eternal life is not a mere hope, because we have a reason for the hope that is in us.

Perhaps the most rational beginning is an effort to see whether we have, or can have, some hint concerning God's purpose in creating our amazing world. We have a very strong hint in the fact that the created order presents a series of levels. Most of creation appears to be unconscious, unfeeling, and totally without intelligence. This is what Pascal means by the order of bodies. Though we do not know what is going on in other parts of the universe in this particular regard, we do know that on our own planet this order of bodies has been succeeded historically by radically different orders, which we normally call life and mind and spirit. While the lines between these are sometimes hazy, it is nevertheless true that the orders are genuine, since their characteristics differ in kind. The movement from unconsciousness to consciousness to self-consciousness may have been long and gradual, but it has occurred! If any one wishes

---

[5] *Christian Devotion, op. cit.,* p. 113.

to claim that this does not represent advance he is free to do so, but he will not be believed. Self-consciousness does not necessarily develop into goodness, but it represents real novelty in the world, with unpredictable potential.

The thoughtful observer is bound to note, not merely that our world is made up of orders, but also that they have appeared *successively*. The highest orders have appeared last, and are made possible by the existence of the earlier ones. Now the point is that this looks like a purposive development. It looks as though, all along, God had been preparing a setting for the emergence of creatures capable of freely chosen goodness. If the world makes sense at all, and is not a mere mass of confusion, here is something truly intelligible. All the pain and turmoil of creation is justified if it finally makes possible the life of one really good person. The world makes sense if it is a scene for the production of personality.

The conception of meaning just mentioned is that presented in the New Testament. In the crucial passage we are told that "the whole creation has been groaning in travail together until now" (Rom. 8:22), and that all the travail has been ennobled by an evident purpose. This purpose is to "obtain the glorious liberty of the children of God." Though we have a better understanding of the temporal span of the creative process than was available to the author of this eloquent passage, this does not alter the situation at all. In any case the process is a long one, but it is seen as a meaningful one because "the creation waits with eager longing for the revealing of the sons of God" (Rom. 8:19). The long development of the solar system, with the formation of planets, is something about which we form rational hypotheses, but there is one feature which is more than hypothesis: this long process has eventuated in persons who are able to *study* the process. Here we have, not speculation, but unchallenged fact. It is a fact more revealing than are any of the particular

discoveries of human intelligence, or all of them put together.

The Christian is one who takes this evident development
seriously and understands it as a development which has a
meaning. Though we cannot know exactly what God is like,
we are convinced that He is like Christ, and Christ, we know,
cared for persons. We have reason to believe that God cares
for persons because He has made a world in which they can
live and learn and, though they are often wrong, discover that
they *are* wrong. We do not know, absolutely, that God's
purpose is that of making possible the "glorious liberty" of
His children, but we at least know that no other purpose is
even being suggested. The only live alternative to this is that
the world has no meaning at all, but if this is true, all effort
at understanding anything is ultimately futile anyway. The
Christian is one who believes that it is not futile.

The next step in the logic of belief is to see what follows
from acceptance of God's valuation of persons. Is it likely
that the divine purpose, which has been worked out with
such patience, will be frustrated in the end? The crucial
point to make is that, if the death of the body means the end
of self-consciousness, then the evident purpose is being defeated. If a person who has learned and suffered for fifty years
is suddenly cut off, with no continuation individually, from
what he has learned about living, and with no further opportunity to love, the absurdity is really too great to be believed.

Plato did not put the argument in exactly this way, but it
is clear that it was the absurdity of an end to Socrates that
most convinced him of the reality of immortality. A world,
he thought, in which the goodness of Socrates could be
utterly destroyed by drinking a little poison, was simply
unintelligible. Plato, it must be remembered, was not primarily concerned about *himself;* his belief in immortality
was not the projection of his own desire; it was the destruc-
tion of his teacher that seemed so unreasonable.

The Christian faith is not Platonism, though Christians are glad to learn from Plato, but both Christianity and Platonism agree upon the irrationality of bodily death as final. Both realize that the higher orders make use of the lower orders in earthly existence, but both deny that the higher orders are ultimately dependent upon the lower. How consciousness will be possible, and is possible for Socrates now, we do not know, of course, but we are greatly helped by noting the progress that occurs in the earthy life of such a man, whose mind becomes more the master than the servant of the body. Life after death, whatever else it may be, is reasonable if it is a completion of a process already begun here. "It may be said, indeed," said Socrates, "that without bones and muscles and the other parts of the body I cannot execute my purposes. But to say that I do as I do because of them, and that this is the way in which mind acts, and not from the choice of the best, is a very careless and idle mode of speaking."[6]

It is fortunate that belief in life after death does not depend upon a sentimental estimate of human goodness, since goodness is often conspicuous by its absence. It depends, instead, on human *promise*. Disappointing as human life may be, and often is, it gives evidence of being intrinsically an unfinished business, for something is begun which requires completion for its very significance. All this makes sense if we are getting ready for something more glorious than anything which we now know. If it is a fulfillment, and not merely a continuation or repetition, it will necessarily be as different from what we now experience as consciousness is different from mere life. This is the meaning of the biblical affirmation that "the sufferings of this present time are not worth comparing with the glory that is to be revealed to us" (Rom. 8:18).

As was said earlier in this book, the Christian's faith in life everlasting is, for the most part, a consequential faith. It fol-

6 *Phaedo,* 99A.

lows from faith in God, whose purpose we think will not be
defeated by anything as small as the cessation of a heartbeat.
Our method is still the method of Socrates, which he described as follows: "I first assumed some principle which I
judged to be the strongest, and then I affirmed as true
whatever seemed to agree with this."[7] This is also the Christian method. The Christian finds that life everlasting is in
agreement with the conception of God which he has been
led, on other grounds, to adopt.

One of the most convincing intellectual supports of the
belief that the death of the body is not the end of the story is
one which, unfortunately, is little understood or employed.
This is the support that comes from a serious acceptance of
the problem of evil, a problem which occurs to almost all
people when they observe the vast amount of unmerited and
even unredemptive suffering in the world. It is important to
remember that this is not a problem for the convinced
atheist, who does not believe in a meaningful order anyway;
but it is a serious problem for one who believes that God is
and that He is like Christ. All who deal with either the philosophy of religion or Christian theology try to handle this
dilemma, but there is never perfect success, for while some
angles of it may be reduced in sharpness, the problem itself
remains.

Contrary to what is often assumed, the Christian seeks not
to deny the apparent injustice in the world, but rather to face
it in its most challenging form. The curious consequence of
this procedure is that there emerges from it one of the
strongest reasons we have for affirming life after death, an
argument which received one of its best expressions in the
thought of Dr. Samuel Johnson.[8] The gist of it is as follows:

---

7 *Phaedo*, 100A.

8 Johnson's statement was: "Since the common events of the present life
happen alike to the good and bad, it follows from the justice of the Supreme
Being that there must be another state of existence in which a just retribution
shall be made."

If God really is, and if He is in a meaningful sense fully sovereign in His universe, He cannot be defeated in His loving purpose. In the words of Micah, this purpose, in which reverent men join, includes both justice and mercy. But if this life is all there is, then justice and mercy are denied to millions. Those who have died by torture are not really less deserving of happiness than I am. If death ends all, we are forced to conclude that for many life is an unmitigated tragedy and thus constitutes a concrete denial of God's individual care. If, on the other hand, this life is not all, justice may still be done. Without the life everlasting the problem of evil is as insoluble as it is damaging to faith in God; *with* life everlasting, divine justice is possible. We cannot, if we believe in God at all, believe in His defeat; therefore we believe that there is another and fuller life in which the justice that is denied here may be finally achieved.

I shall never forget the sense of intellectual relief which came to my mind when I began to consider seriously the twin mysteries of "arrival" and "survival." I was puzzled, as is every one who thinks about the matter, by the problem of how consciousness can be possible without the nervous system. I had good reason to be aware of the fact that, if a surgeon cuts away part of the human brain, there is consequent loss of mental powers. If consciousness is thus dependent, as it seems to be, upon a material substance, how can it go on if that very substance decays and returns to dust, as it surely will.

This problem has not ceased to worry me, but I have been helped, immeasurably, by the consideration of a companion problem. How could it be that, in a world made up basically of merely material forces, there would ever arise a being who is able to be puzzled by the very fact of his being. I saw that here was a mystery, not less great, but even greater than that of the continuation of personal identity after the decay of brain tissue. But the overwhelming fact is that the step from matter to self-consciousness *has actually been taken*. Here the mystery is the mystery of known fact. Self-conscious personality, far from being a leap in the dark, is a leap into the light. It has come! And it has come in the most improbable manner. However great, then, may be the miracle of survival, it is more than matched by the known and already enacted miracle of arrival. More than anything else I know, this turns the edge of the problem.

No Christian can consider the problem of death apart from the resurrection of Jesus Christ. The miracle of history according to which a despised little group survived in the face of both ridicule and persecution is closely associated with Christ's victory over death. This was the central fact to which the early Christians, in a period of sustained vitality unexampled in all history, always appealed. In his famous sermon on Mars Hill in Athens, Paul used the resurrection of Christ as his final effort to reach an unbelieving people. Of Christ he said that God "has given assurance to all men by raising him from the dead" (Acts 17:31). At this some mocked, but others said, "We will hear you again about this." The outcome was that they and others heard the same story over and over. The faith in the resurrection was, consequently, deeply imbedded in the consciousness of the early Christians even before the Gospels were written, and the details of this unique event were fully described.

The resurrection of Christ either occurred or it did not. Every early Christian, so far as we know, believed that it had occurred, but millions in our time, including some who call themselves followers of Christ, believe that it did not. Clearly somebody is wrong! Who is it? Whoever is wrong, we cannot be sorry that there is subjective doubt. The method of doubt, as developed by Descartes and already stressed in this book, is on the whole a beneficent one. How else are we to avoid superstition and self-delusion? When, in his *Autobiography*,

John Stuart Mill was explaining his indebtedness to his wife he said, "It is not the least of my intellectual obligations to her that I have derived from her a wise skepticism." Mill's phrase is an excellent one and draws attention to a mood which we must continue to cultivate. But mere skepticism, however valuable as a beginning, is not satisfactory at the end. Finally, a truly thoughtful person must look at the evidence and try to draw a reasonable conclusion. About such a conclusion he may still feel humble, but it is a person's intellectual duty to reject the least likely of possible alternatives.

This evidence which impressed and convinced the Christians of the first century was that of witnesses. Paul's reference to the cumulative effect of this is so important that it justifies full repetition.

Now I would remind you, brethren, in what terms I preached to you the gospel, which you received, in which you stand, by which you are saved, if you hold it fast—unless you believed in vain. For I delivered unto you as of first importance what I also received, that Christ died for our sins in accordance with the scriptures, that he was buried, that he was raised on the third day in accordance with the scriptures, and that he appeared to Cephas, then to the twelve. Then he appeared to more than five hundred brethren at one time, most of whom are still alive, though some have fallen asleep. Then he appeared to James, then to all the apostles. Last of all, as to one untimely born, he appeared also to me (I Cor. 15:1–9).

What can we say of cumulative evidence of such impressiveness? Though nobody in his senses can neglect it, many think they have a way of escaping it. In the modern world, having moved over from Cartesian doubt to outright denial, a good many tend to say that these witnesses to Christ's resurrection were, though sincere, essentially deluded men.

They *thought* that they had seen Him and had talked with Him, but in this they were mistaken. All that they were reporting was a psychological experience, a fanciful objectification of their inner needs. Others, of course, say that these men and women were undoubtedly reporting a spiritual experience, but that the physical resurrection of Christ's body did not occur. When people are pressed for a reason for this outright rejection of the New Testament witness, cogent answers are seldom given. All that is offered is something to the effect that in this scientific age we now know that such events do not and cannot occur. This answer loses most of its supposed cogency as soon as it is clearly formulated, because it is obviously based on a mere assumption. How do we know what can happen? Science, important as it is, has no logical bearing upon the question at all, except in its encouragement to us to look at the evidence, which is what we ought to do anyway. To say that the resurrection did not occur because it has not occurred elsewhere is to miss entirely the very point of the alleged singularity of this transcendently important event.

In my own life, I certainly began as a skeptic so far as the resurrection of Christ is concerned. I thought of the story as comparable to stories in Greek mythology, and accordingly carried my doubt to the point of denial. I knew, of course, that the early Christians believed that Christ rose, but I was aware of the fact that many people, in many ages, have believed things that are manifestly untrue. The first real change in my conclusion came when I began to consider seriously a particular kind of evidence, that of altered lives. Suddenly I saw that the primary evidence provided by the apostles is not what they *said,* but what they *became.*

At one point in time the erstwhile followers of Christ were a poor little bedraggled band; they were going home because the dream had evaporated. They had believed that, somehow,

Christ was the herald of a new order, but now it was evident that they had been wrong in this judgment, since He had been killed just like any criminal. They were, of course, well aware of the stories of other leaders whose work suddenly came to nothing. "For before these days," said Gamaliel, "Theudas arose, giving himself out to be somebody, and a number of men, about four hundred, joined him; but he was slain and all who followed him were dispersed and came to nothing" (Acts 5:36).

It looked, in that bleak time, as though the same pathetic tragedy had been reenacted. What is more poignant than the remark of the disappointed apostles, "We had hoped that he was the one to redeem Israel" (Luke 24:21)? The enthusiasm of His presence, the shared vitality, the creative hope—all these were gone, and one more bubble had burst. But then another event, and one of a totally different order, began to occur. In a short time these broken men became strong, confident, and bold as lions. They sang; they rejoiced; they healed; they taught; they suffered triumphantly. And this they did, not only for a few days of passing enthusiasm, but for all the remainder of their lives. They faced persecution and even death with a triumphant spirit that baffled their tormentors. A characteristic account is the following: "So they took his advice, and when they had called in the apostles, they beat them and charged them not to speak in the name of Jesus, and let them go. Then they left the presence of the council, rejoicing that they were counted worthy to suffer dishonor for the name. And every day in the temple and at home they did not cease teaching and preaching Jesus as the Christ" (Acts 5:40–42).

Now the serious student must seek an explanation for a change so revolutionary and so enduring. What was the sufficient cause? To this the early Christians gave their own answer: *it happened, they asserted, solely because Christ arose from the dead.* He talked with them, so that their hearts burned within them. Since the best evidence is found in consequences rather than in mere words, it is hard to think of events in ancient history for which the verification is more compelling.

Though I am not sure, it may be that my attention was first drawn to this type of evidence by my reading of Pascal. I admired his firmness of mind when he wrote that the apostles were either deceived or deceivers. But what struck me most was the emphasis upon the importance of the *act*. "While Jesus Christ was with them, He could sustain them. But, after that, if He did not appear to them, who inspired them to act?"[9] In his notations about proof, Pascal's major observation was:

The supposition that the apostles were imposters is very absurd. Let us think it out. Let us imagine those twelve men, assembled after the death of Jesus Christ, plotting to say that He was risen. By this they attack all the powers. The heart of man is strangely inclined to fickleness, to change, to promises, to gain. However little any of them might have been led astray by all these attractions, nay more, by the fear of prisons, tortures, and death, they were lost. Let us follow up this thought.[10]

Though we are sorry that Blaise Pascal did not live to follow up the thought, we can see with some assurance the direction in which he would have moved. Dismissing the hypothesis that the apostles were conscious deceivers, he needed next to ask whether they were deceived. This is the relevant question now, because modern man usually tries to solve the dilemma in this way. The apostles, we like to say, were good men, but they were also gullible and without the advantage of knowing psychology. Their change in behavior

9 *Pensées*, No. 801.
10 *Ibid.* No. 800.

was simply an evidence of mass delusion. However easy this is to say, it is full of intellectual difficulties. Have we any other illustration of mass delusion on this scale, for such a period of time, and with such ethical consequences? To call it mass delusion is really to make the upholder of the hypothesis seem the gullible person. Has he let a dogma blind him to the facts of changed lives? This is the point of J. B. Phillips when he says, "It is surely straining credulity to bursting point to believe that this dramatic and sustained change of attitude was founded on hallucination, hysteria, or an ingenious swindle."[11]

We must remember, when we ask whether the resurrection did or did not occur, that those who first heard of the event, including some of the disciples, were properly skeptical. Refusing simply to take a man's word for it they required something more, and the fact is that they got it. This sort of evidence is likely to appeal to any man's intelligence, unless he has already erected such a barrier that he will not listen. The conventional barrier, that of physical impossibility, depends in turn upon an assumption that no man has a right to make. In a world of such wonder as ours is, why should it seem incredible that the loving purpose of the Living God would find expression in a truly unique event, designed to bring healing and hope to all men?

The resurrection is indeed a miracle, but miracles are possible unless ours is a closed universe. Though we have long accepted the epigram of Thomas Chalmers that "the uniformity of nature is but another name for the faithfulness of God," we know that unexampled events do occur. Christians, fortunately, have a philosophy big enough to enable them to refer unique events to the same Source as more familiar occurrences. An undogmatic philosophy leaves room for the resurrection of Christ to occur, while a careful study

11 *Your God Is Too Small, op. cit.,* p. 112.

of the evidence leads to the conclusion that it *did* occur. The consequence is that death is neither so fearsome nor so final as we have tended to suppose.

Though every worshiper who repeats the Apostles' Creed is familiar with the phrase, "the resurrection of the body," there is reason to suppose that it is perplexing to many, including even those who are personally devout. The expression refers to ourselves. By the resurrection of the body Christians, from the earliest times, have meant that in the life that succeeds our experience here, individuals will retain their personal identity. Since the body is, in this life, a means of distinguishing one individual from another, the conviction is that in the future life there will be an analogue. Otherwise we should lose that which is intrinsic to personality, its *singularity*. Christ taught that each one is precious, but if personal identity is lost, what Christ prized will also be lost. Our conviction, as Christians, is that it will not be lost.

No Christian claims to know exactly what the analogue of the physical body will be in the life everlasting. Paul struggled with the problem and called it a "spiritual body," but he distinguished this clearly from a "physical body" such as each living person now occupies. The one thing sure, then, is that the resurrection of the body, which Christians so confidently affirm in their creed, does not refer to "flesh." As though to avoid confusion on this point Paul wrote, "I tell you this, brethren; flesh and blood cannot inherit the kingdom of God" (I Cor. 15:50).

We have a slight hint of how great a change is possible in a person's means of identification, by considering the body of the Risen Christ. Though the risen body was, as it had been before the crucifixion, the means by which He was identifiable, it also exhibited certain characteristics which were totally new. For example, this body could go through a wall and disappear, yet at the same time the marks of the nails were clearly visible. Here we are in the realm of the mysterious, but that ought not to bother us. Of course it is not simple, but what right have we to suppose that the *truth* is simple? We have only begun to learn! If Christ, when He arose, exhibited something midway between human flesh and a spiritual body, why not, like Thomas Huxley, sit down before the fact like a little child?[12]

The idea that our earthly bodies, which are made of flesh, will continue to exist eternally, is so preposterous that reverent believers have regularly rejected it. One reason why it is preposterous is that such a continuation would perpetuate rather than correct the injustices of this life. For the hunchback to be eternally a hunchback would be a mark, not of heaven, but of hell! Only if such inequities are transcended can the redeeming love of Christ be exemplified.

Thinking people ought to be neither surprised nor puzzled to learn that, when Christians refer to the resurrection of their bodies, they are employing a figure of speech. No one supposes that, when Christ says that He is the Door, He is made of *wood*. The truth is that the deepest truths cannot be communicated except in figures. While the term "body" is manifestly inadequate in reference to the future life, it is reasonable for us to employ it, because any alternative we can think of is *less* adequate. But when we use it we have a responsibility to explain it, so as to reduce confusion as far as possible.

The point to which we must return again and again is that, in our conviction that the decay of the flesh is not a final event, we must meticulously avoid reference to a vague spirituality. There may be in store for us something better than what we know of personality, but we may be assured that this new life will at least be personal. Though we know that "we

---

[12] In this connection, see the interesting observations of Charles Davis in *A Question of Conscience, op. cit.*, p. 164.

shall be changed," we have good reason to suppose that the love of Christ will not change and that it will dignify our little lives, however different they may be from anything we now experience. Now we see through a glass, darkly, but then we shall see face to face. In this life we are forced to live by faith; in the life to come we shall live, not by faith, but by open vision.